Antiques Professional Secrets for the Amateur

Michel Doussy comes from a long line of artisans and himself started cabinet making at the age of thirteen. He has been a journalist for many years and is a regular broadcaster on television and radio on the subject of do-it-yourself.

M. Doussy lives in Paris with his wife and two children.

Michel Doussy

ANTIQUES

Professional Secrets for the Amateur

translated from the French by Patrick Evans

Pan Books London and Sydney

First published in Great Britain 1973 by Souvenir Press Ltd
and simultaneously in Canada by J. M. Dent & Sons (Canada) Ltd
This edition published 1976 by Pan Books Ltd,
Cavaye Place, London SW10 9PG
© Editions Stock 1971
English Translation © 1973 Patrick Evans
ISBN 0 330 24809 X
Printed and bound in Great Britain by
Richard Clay (The Chaucer Press) Ltd, Bungay, Suffolk

To my father, an art-craftsman
To my son, who takes after him

Hydrogen peroxide In the term Hydrogen Peroxide
(120 vols), the bracketed quantity means that for, say, every
teaspoon of a solution of the mixture, 120 teaspoonfuls of oxygen
are released by effervescence as the mixture disintegrates.

Contents

Preface

This book by Michel Doussy eludes the clutches of literary criticism or art criticism; it is not in their province. It bobs gaily and humorously along; it is akin to the works of practical information which have been appearing ever since the late fifteenth century, when the Florentine Cenino Cenini, to combat boredom while in prison for debt, wrote a treatise on the painting and restoration of pictures.

Some of Michel Doussy's ancestors were *compagnons du Tour de France* – craftsmen who, after completing their apprenticeship, had travelled the country plying their trade and increasing their knowledge; his undertaking reflects something of their simple, almost naïve, attitude. It is as if he had been commissioned to restore the objects collected by *le facteur* Cheval the postman and *amateur*, whose eccentric hoard is now on the way to fame – and had felt impelled thereafter to turn instructor. Specialized craftsmen may smile at his summary treatment; in a few pages he gives directions for repairing a piece of furniture, nursing its veneers and pegs, restoring its gilding. In the same way, collectors of bronzes, or lovers of jewellery or Renaissance ceramics, will look down their noses at an author who in a few short chapters presumes to expound the various cuts of rock crystal, or the repair of faïences and porcelains.

The fact remains that this is a well-informed book. Michel Doussy knows his subject and his easily applied recipes will restore the bloom to many a jaded *bibelot*. Here is encouragement for youthful amateurs, many of them with slim purses, to venture out into the provinces and try their luck among the small antique dealers, seeking that beauty and delight which are the reward of a successful discovery. Unfortunately, the relatively low market value of many of these finds prevents the amateur from entrusting them to an expert craftsman for repair. With the help of this book he will learn like a family which has adopted a child how to look after them, nurse them in sickness, protect them from the maladies which attack wood, bronze and other materials. He will not only save money on costly repairs; he will give himself the extra pleasure of becoming intimately acquainted with his purchase, and of imbuing it with the aura of his own passion.

Finally, it is to be hoped that this book will awaken in a few readers a vocation for the restoration of *objets d'art*: a fascinating profession which demands years of apprenticeship but, quite rightly, is among the best-paid of all categories of manual work. Specialists in these lines charge high fees; the monthly income of a front-rank craftsman is in many cases equal to that of a higher civil servant, or someone at middle management level.

The book is largely instructional in character. The author knows how to teach by entertaining; he hops merrily from one subject to another and, by means of an apparent disorder which is in fact perfectly deliberate, holds the reader's attention. This is something which the qualified expert, with his specialized approach, does not always find easy to achieve.

Maurice Rheims

Foreword

There are dynasties of antique dealers, just as there used to be dynasties of cabinet makers or painters. Does this mean that personal aptitude is a matter of genetic inheritance? Our own opinion is that the transmission, from generation to generation, of techniques and knowledge – including 'secrets', naturally – has been of great value to the descendants of truly creative individuals. But where does art fit into this process? The question can be answered only by someone capable of formulating the relationship of art to technique, and of telling us how much either owes to the other.

Why do I put antique dealers in the same category as the cabinet makers and painters – the artists? Simply because everything ends up in the antique dealer's shop; not only the artists' material creations but also a thorough knowledge of technique; *all* the techniques. We can hardly quarrel with the antique dealers for jealously guarding what they know. Familiarity with old furniture and other objects of value requires a mass of observation and experience, built up on a foundation of genuine culture. An accumulation of knowledge presupposes an ally: time. And this, in turn, means predecessors.

It is true most antique dealers are self-taught, but would they themselves claim that they had never regretted the absence of an expert guide in the early stages? His presence would have enabled them to bypass a forest of mistakes and hesitations.

It was with all these thoughts in mind that I set out to write the book. While planning and putting it together I saw myself in imagination confronted by a Dutch or Spanish cabinet, with the lid open and a multitude of drawers all empty, awaiting use. In each of them I was to place a few particles of knowledge, guided by my own experience, my likes and dislikes, my personal inquiries, and finally to check the whole by consultation with qualified specialists.

Having brought my manuscript to an arbitrary close – otherwise it might never have reached the public – I left the imaginary cabinet open, with its compartments more or less filled but some of them still empty. Why? There's a first time for everything, and while I am aware that none of the drawers will ever be completely full I can at least claim credit for having tried.

Not everyone is going to thank me.

A well-known dealer told me what his father used to impress on him: 'When a customer comes in, shake hands with him but don't say anything – because, you see, in our trade, by just saying "Good morning" you've already said too much.'

This secretiveness and love of mystery have, for many years past, constituted the armour-plating round the financial well-being of a small, select profession. Today, however, the trade has 'come down into the market-place'. Census figures show a total of 3000 antique dealers and junk dealers in Paris and about 7000 in the provinces, and the clientele too has democratically broadened out and diversified. Today's 'young Turks' no longer gamble on the customer's ignorance; on the contrary, they like their customers to be well-informed, to understand what is being offered to them, and not to grudge paying a fair price for it. So 'secrets' are out of date; their time has run out.

But in watching one profession develop, we are also witnessing the irrevocable death of another: that of the restorer of antiques. Marc Roy, founder of the Guide Emer, the Bible of antique and curio dealers all over France, states that the youngest restorers are all over sixty and that most of them are between seventy and eighty-five. What is worse is that they are alone, without apprentices to carry on after they are gone. Every time one of them dies it is like the destruction of capital; his knowledge dies with him. A few specialists, however, have undertaken the essential task of composing a methodical survey of the arts of restoration. The most skilful of them all is probably André France-Lanord, founder of the Laboratory of Archaeological Research at the Musée Lorrain in Nancy. It was he who recon-stituted the crater of Vix, saved the horses of St Mark's in Venice, and achieved the improbable feats of restoring the statue of Pacatianus at Vienne (Isère) and the clothes and jewellery of the Merovingian queen Arnegonde, whose body had lain under the flagstones of the church of Saint-Denis from the sixth century to our own day. He, if anyone, is aware that unless restorers get together and exchange information, an incalculable number of relics from the past will be lost for ever.

In his opinion, this exchange should be executed systematically: after every repair, the details should be noted on a record-card which will thereafter accompany the piece on its journey through space and time. Thus, whenever a great craftsman dies only his own marvellous touch and skill will go with him; his technique, substantially, will remain with us. What is doubtful is whether all the craftsmen will be easy to convince of the need to communicate their knowledge; and, equally, whether we can educate the public sufficiently, so that they can apply first-aid themselves whenever they have a piece which they cannot afford to entrust to a specialist. A badly repaired piece is surely better than none at all.

In this book we have attempted to draw the line at which do-it-yourself repairs should halt, and to prevent a number of mistakes. There are certain time-honoured but unscientific procedures we did not feel obliged to disclaim; many of them are both effective and safe. There are picturesque recipes, some of which seem highly fanciful, but which, empirical though they are, rational analysis has not condemned. It took a forger, van Meegeren, to discover that Vermeer painted his canvases with oil of lilac; deterioration in *Le Moulin de la Galette* revealed that Renoir did not know how to prepare a canvas; and only when the ceiling painted by Chagall for the Paris Opéra began steadily coming away was it discovered that the painting of his predecessor, Jules Lenepveu, which Chagall had used as a ground for his own, had been executed with a beeswax base to armour it against the fumes from the gas-lights of the principal chandelier.

In an age like ours, can we really tolerate having to learn the 'secrets' of art the hard way, or by chance?

This book sets out hopefully to fill the gap, and to initiate a dialogue between those who know and those who seek.

1 Adhesives

Adhesives: tabulated information

Materials	Adhesives recommended	Points to watch
All species of wood. Carcase wood, joints, ply, insulating board, compressed wall-board	Vinyl adhesives Fish glue Casein	Cramp parts together Beware of damp For rough surfaces, oily woods, low temperatures. May stain wood
Wide areas of contact in any material. Fibre board, veneers. Laminates.	Neoprene contact adhesives	Coat both surfaces and allow to dry for a few minutes before contact
Plastic tiles, mural sheets, plastic floor coverings. Anti-damp coverings (insulating or foil-backed board)	Acrylic adhesives	Same technique, but position of parts can be adjusted after contact, before adhesive sets
Joints intended to resist humidity, water or hydrocarbons	Resorcinol adhesives and plastic resins	Temperature not less than 15 °C (59 °F). Follow makers' directions closely; they vary, but are always essential to produce the required chemical reaction. Don't use resorcinol adhesives on porous surfaces. If necessary apply a second coat after the first has dried

Materials	Adhesives recommended	Points to watch
Polyvinyl Polyethylene Plastic floor tiles	Solvent-based adhesives	Coat both surfaces thinly; allow to dry before contact. Avoid bubbles or air pockets
Expanded polystyrene	Special mastics Synthetic resins	Apply in blobs These behave like neoprene but do not dissolve expanded polystyrene
	Certain vinyl adhesives	Ask manufacturers about the characteristics of these
Glass, enamel, metal, faïence, marble	Epoxy resins	Use in atmosphere of not less than 15 °C. Coat both surfaces and let them partially dry. Remove superfluous resin with alcohol before it sets. NB There is a one-part contact variety
Textiles Wallpaper, cardboard	Latex adhesives Starch adhesives Cellulose adhesives	Contact only required Dissolve in water Dissolve in water; allow to stand for thirty minutes before use

Modern adhesives are revolutionizing traditional skills

Of all the numerous discoveries placed at the disposal of antique restorers in recent years those of the adhesives industry, with its plastic resins and special solvents, are undoubtedly the most astonishing. But technical progress, it should be remembered, is always a matter of specialization. Grandad's famous old glue, his stand-by for everything from joinery to marquetry to bookbinding, has been ousted not by one product but by ten.

The following principal uses of modern adhesives may therefore not be out of place.

Wood

For all ordinary joints – tenon-and-mortise, butt joints, dovetail, half-lap joints, etc. – *vinyl adhesives*, as a rule, will do.

These white or transparent liquids, with a pleasant smell and a long shelf life (which makes them practical for occasional use), stand up to moisture pretty well but are unhappy at low temperatures, which cause them to dry slowly and stick badly.

Many manufacturers have improved their vinyl glues by adding special ingredients which (or so they tell us) produce an all-purpose adhesive, suitable for concrete, leather, plastics, laminates and so on. We shall come back to this when reviewing these materials individually; for the moment we shall confine ourselves to general guidance. Vinyl adhesives are very powerful when used thinly. They cannot be recommended for joining irregular surfaces requiring a thick layer of glue. Some of them set quickly, others take longer, but as a general rule it is advisable to apply a reasonable amount of pressure to the joint so as to ensure a thin strong film.

*

Never prematurely subject a joint to the load it is going to have to bear; it is always safer to wait for twenty-four hours.

Warning! Beware of vinyl glues which separate into several layers; they are usually badly balanced emulsions and in any case deficient in vinyl, owing their viscosity to the addition of talc, which naturally tends to sink and form a deposit. Glues of this nature lack quality.

Fish glue, where wood is concerned, cannot be overlooked. It has one grave defect: it does not stand up to damp. It smells unpleasant but holds well; however, its day is really over.

Casein glues, on the other hand, are old-fashioned but still far from obsolete for certain special purposes, notably for working in cold weather and for use on oily varieties of wood. You may not know that most of the exotic woods, such as teak, lignum vitae, South American rosewood and hickory, exude oily substances which interfere with adhesion (before gluing or painting any of these, clean the surface with trichlo or white spirit). Some resinous woods, such as red pine and yew, have the same peculiarity. Casein destroys the exuded substance and makes work with these woods possible. Moreover, casein is effective on irregular surfaces, because it does not shrink when drying and keeps its strength when put on thickly, even on badly made joints. Cramps should therefore be only lightly applied, so as to avoid squeezing out the glue; their only purpose is to maintain the contact.

Drawbacks of casein: it is vulnerable to damp, and some kinds of wood, such as oak and mahogany, are discoloured by it.

Wood responds well to every type of glue, but special cases frequently occur. For example, the question of fibreboard or compressed wallboard panels, which you certainly won't encounter in old furniture but which you may want to use for lining a cupboard. A good general rule is to stick them with a vinyl adhesive, laying it on a little thicker than usual to allow for the porous quality of the material. Alternatively, neoprene glues – 'contact' adhesives as they are called, because cramping is unnecessary – are suitable. The pieces being joined become totally inseparable the moment they are brought into contact. To obtain this effect, *both* surfaces must be glued: each is given a very thin film of adhesive and allowed to dry until it will no longer stick to the fingers. Only then are they brought together; adhesion is ensured by striking here and there with a hammer and with a piece of wood to mask the blows and prevent marking.

Neoprene is best suited to sticking large surfaces which give its limpet-like quality full scope. The following are its main uses:

1. Fibreboard panels.

2. Laminates (superimposed on wood).

3. Veneering; neoprene makes this much easier, particularly on curved surfaces. The bulky old veneering presses are now totally unnecessary. Traditional cabinet makers distrust neoprene but this may be merely lack of familiarity.

4. Finally, surfaces which are damp themselves and are going to be exposed to damp after covering with another material. The highly volatile solvents incorporated in neoprene adhesives evaporate on coming into contact with water and make it possible to apply the covering material in conditions which would defeat any other type of adhesive.

Another class of special cases: resistance to fresh or salt water and, in some circumstances, to hydrocarbons (as in the moulds used in boatbuilding); a field which calls for *resorcinol* adhesives or for *plastic resins*, both of which usually consist of two separate substances.

Plastic resins are cheaper than resorcinol. They are usually in the form of a powder (ureaformaldehyde) and a catalyst. Some manufacturers specify their being mixed with water, others with a special solvent. The resulting joint is of almost mineral hardness. Follow the manufacturer's directions carefully.

The observation most frequently made is that these adhesives require a certain degree of warmth – not less than 15 °C – in order to 'take' properly.

Another observation from experience is that the joints on which adhesives of this type are used should be very exact or else should not be subjected to movement and stress. The film, which, as already indicated, is very hard, may also be brittle, especially if it is thick.

*

To avoid making this chapter overspecialized, and omitting to specify some of the modern types of adhesive on the ground that they are of no interest to the restorer, we have drawn up the chart on pages 15–16.

Plastics

There is no need to emphasize the role of plastics for wall coverings, floorings, household articles and so on. The exploiting of these new materials has demanded the creation of special adhesives: some solvents 'burn' some plastics or, alternatively, simply inhibit adhesion.

Every kind of plastic covering will accept neoprene glue (a thicker grade is used for this). But *acrylic adhesives* should not be overlooked: their one advantage over neoprene is that surfaces stuck together can be shifted about while the drying (which is not instantaneous) is still incomplete. Thus one has a few minutes' grace in which to rectify an error when using plastic or porcelain tiles, for instance.

On *polyvinyl* and *polyethylene*, solvent-based adhesives are very suitable. Spread the adhesive thinly on both surfaces, leave it for a few minutes while the solvent evaporates and then bring them together, avoiding air pockets. Finish off by rubbing vigorously.

Be careful with expanded *polystyrene*: it is the odd man out in the plastics family. Most solvents attack it. It is fixed either with a special mastic put on in blobs about the size of a walnut or hazel nut (at the four corners of a sheet about 30 cm × 30 cm, for example), or with synthetic resins. The latter 'take' instantly, like adhesives.

Glass, enamel, metal, faïence and *marble* are best suited by epoxy resins. These are expensive but will stand up to just about everything, including temperatures of 300 °C and considerable mechanical strain.

We recommend double gluing (i.e. coat both surfaces), and partial drying before contact. Any adhesive squeezed out of the join should be carefully wiped off with spirits while the resin is still liquid.

Textiles

These have entered interior decoration in a big way, as tapestries and wall hangings. Latex adhesives, one of the industry's most successful creations, are just the thing for instant hemming, attaching edgings, repairing canvases or putting on patches. Usually supplied in handy dispensers, they stick at once, by contact alone. It no longer makes sense to use the old-fashioned methods now that we have latex adhesives (which also stick leather).

Finally, the best adhesives for *paper* and *cardboard* are still *starch* glues (soluble in water), or *cellulose* glues (which should be dissolved in water and left to stand for half an hour).

2 Amber

♥

Amber

Amber is simply the resin of fossilized conifers. Highly prized in the Near, Middle and Far East and throughout Islam, the *elektron* of the Greeks originates in the Baltic Sea. It is known with certainty that, from the earliest epochs of mankind, amber has been used as a currency and, of course, for personal adornment. According to a belief still widely held today, it possesses therapeutic and antibiotic qualities in every kind of illness or emotional disturbance. Necklaces made of bits of unworked amber threaded on silk ribbon are placed round the necks of newborn babies and little children because, or so it seems, this ensures teething without tears. To the end of his days, Sacha Guitry ostentatiously wore a necklace of large beads of amber, and frequently informed his family of his conviction that this long, voluminous necklace possessed the virtue of recharging his energy. Such are the beliefs which have attached themselves to amber.

The Far East, in particular, has always carved figures of members of its philosophical and religious pantheon in blocks of amber, and is still exporting them via Hong Kong.

At this point we must warn the amateur to be very much on his guard: amber is rarely, practically never, absolutely pure; as we have indicated, it consists of the resinous exudations from giant conifers which perished in the geological upheavals of the Tertiary Period. Hence vegetable fragments and fossil insects of several hundreds of species were embedded in it. One naturally raises an eyebrow when being shown carved figures, sometimes as much as 50 cm high, of perfect transparency and purity, in which the most careful examination can find no flaw. The vendor will perhaps try to make out that the piece is worth a lot precisely because of its 'exceptional' purity; but don't be too trusting; this is one of the many fields in which a precious material is tending to be replaced by plastics.

Moreover, there is nothing to stop anyone who has mastered the technique of casting with synthetic resins from incorporating insects or vegetable fragments; though, as it happens, this is something that fakers have not attempted – yet.

More widespread, but equally dubious, is a practice which the Chinese have developed with astonishing perfection: melting the stuff down. From amber chips, which are worth little, they produce blocks of considerable size and absolute purity. Sometimes they produce a decorative piece by casting and then dexterously touching it up.

How to recognize amber

Most amber comes from the southern shores of the Baltic. Small quantities are also found in Spain, Italy, Sicily, Syria, Poland and European Russia. Only by chemical analysis can the differences be formally established, and even then not altogether. It has been found that Baltic amber contains a higher proportion of succinic acid than that from elsewhere.

From the earliest times, two varieties of amber have been recognized: *light*, which is the colour of honey or beeswax (the *elektron* of the Greeks), and *dark*, which is reddish brown, like caramel (*suali ternicum*). This distinction indicates nothing about provenance; both kinds are found in the same deposits.

To tell whether a specimen of amber is real or imitation, check first whether it possesses that power of electrical attraction, so mysterious to the ancients, which has always astonished the on-looker and to which our language owes the word 'electricity' (from *electron*). On rubbing the amber with a piece of dry woollen rag, it will be seen that the resulting static electricity attracts dust or tiny bits of paper.

It is true that some kinds of plastic have the same property, but if you sniff the amber after rubbing it you will notice a definite aroma of pine resin.

Repairing amber

There is a very simple method for mending any amber object which is perfectly successful. Daub the broken surfaces with wet caustic soda or caustic potash, press the two (or more) parts together with elastic bands, sticky tape or a weight, and leave for twenty-four hours. The join will then hold.

To *clean* amber is perfectly easy. Use alcohol. Immersion, where possible, is the best method for articles which have got very dirty, such as cigarette-holders. The alcohol will dry almost without trace. If it leaves a thin white deposit, rub the amber with a piece of chamois leather.

Renovating amber

Several things can render amber opaque, the most important of which are time, neglect and exposure to damp. Very ancient pieces, brought to light by excavation, are usually in a state of degeneration and have a dull, dead appearance.

This is how to 'refresh' amber and restore it to its pristine transparency:

If it is dusty, brush it. Never wash the object.

Before starting treatment, make sure the object is perfectly dry. If necessary, leave it in a warm room for a few days (but be careful: do not expose it to direct heat. It is enough to keep it in an atmosphere which is warm and above all dry).

In a suitable vessel, prepare the following mixture:

4 parts rectified turpentine
1 part alcohol (96 per cent)

Suspend the object *above* the liquid and close the vessel, making sure that it is absolutely airtight. After twenty four hours the amber will have completely regained its transparency.

Amber pieces of venerable age deserve to be protected and 'fed'. Mix one part powdered dammar gum with three parts turpentine; add 2 per cent of pure beeswax (mixed in cold, not melted). This mixture is the basis of a series of dilutions which must be carried out successively.

The mixture will be further diluted with turpentine at each stage of the treatment, the proportion of turpentine being decreased by five parts each time, yielding fifteen parts of turpentine, then ten, then five. The final proportion is three parts.

The treatment takes about a month, but the results are spectacular. At each stage, immerse the article completely for two hours, then dry it for three days in a warm dry atmosphere; do this four or five times, always allowing the full drying-out period. In the final bath (three parts turpentine), carry out three or four immersions, with the usual drying-out periods between.

As you see, the treatment is simple. Bear in mind that the results far outweigh the trouble and enable one to rescue pieces of great value.

After at least a fortnight, during which the article can be put back on display, you may polish it gently with a soft, supple chamois leather.

Note: amber can be efficiently protected by giving it a thin coat of cellulose varnish, which will be invisible after application. Varnish should only be applied after reconditioning as described here.

3 Bronze

Bronze

Bronze has been known to man from remote antiquity, as can be seen from the modern name for a major division of prehistory, the Bronze Age. It probably emerged as a chance discovery, since in those times the ores of copper and tin were mixed together and smelted directly. The 'tin' of the ancients was produced in this way. The art of bronze-founding, which was developed in Mesopotamia and Egypt some three thousand years before Christ, was flourishing in Crete by about 2000 B.C. As yet, archaeologists have discovered only small figures (statuettes) in Crete, which implies that large ones were the exception. The big classical bronzes, such as the Zeus of the Artemision and the ephebus of Anticythera, are few, but there are a great many small figures, reliefs and domestic utensils which were finished with the chisel and embellished by the addition of gold or silver.

The Western World, discovering Far Eastern art in the nineteenth century, became aware for the first time of the exceptional quality of Chinese, Korean and Japanese bronzes, and of their antiquity: bronze vessels have been found as far back as the Chang dynasty (fifteenth century B.C.). In Japan, however, it was only towards the third century A.D. that works of art in bronze appeared in abundance and variety: vessels, mirrors and drums, including the famous drums in the temple of Karagor. The Japanese sculptors went on to achieve an art of infinite refinement in their colossal figures; the most celebrated example is the *Trinity* of Kodo.

As for the Romans, they summoned to their aid the best artists in Greece, who, among other things, embellished the Circus in Rome with more than 3000 statues. Today, in Naples Museum, there are 115 bronze sculptures and a large number of articles of furniture, excavated from the ruins of Pompeii.

Information about the bronze-founders of the Middle Ages is scanty. The few known names include those of Jean de Dinant, who signed the lectern in the cathedral at Tongres, in Belgium, and Laurent Urim, who cast Louis XI's tomb.

It is stated, not altogether correctly, that the knowledge of the master bronze-founders of antiquity had perished by the Middle Ages and that there was no longer anyone capable of casting the colossal statues which were the pride of ancient Rome. The Renaissance, with its love of architectural ornament, made many attempts to rediscover the lost art. France, however, seems not to have been interested in this reawakening. Anecdotal tradition maintains that Benvenuto Cellini achieved the masterly rediscovery of the forgotten skills and presented them to the world by casting his celebrated figure of Perseus. This rather overlooks his most famous predecessors, such as his master, Michelangelo, and Verrocchio and, in the Middle Ages, the anonymous Mosan bronze-founders to whom we owe the door at Hildesheim and the cathedral door at Gnesen, those incomparable bronze monuments cast in a single pour in each case, as long ago as the tenth and eleventh centuries.

The leading figure in the revival of bronze-founding in the Renaissance was a Frenchman, Giovanni di Bologna, whose real name was Jean de Boulogne and who was born at Douai. It was not until the seventeenth century that bronze began appearing as a component in furniture, with the advent of Charles-André Boulle. During the eighteenth century bronze was adapted to furniture making: bronze, in the form of handles, rings, locks and mouldings, became the indispensable partner of exotic woods. It was also used in the ornamentation of clocks and candelabra. Artists abounded, masters of their period as well as their art: Caffieri, Duplessis, August Galliène, Leblanc, Saint-Germain, Martincourt and Gouthière, perhaps the most famous of them all. Only one outstanding English bronze founder in the whole of the eighteenth century can be placed beside this list of French masters of the craft: Matthew Boulton of Birmingham (1728–1809) who made ormolu door handles, mounts for giant urns of Blue John or Derbyshire spar, and decorative pieces of furniture. It should be noted, however, that, master though he was of the craft, he still found it necessary to bring in workmen from France to assist him.

In the last century, bronze went out of fashion but today, it is being rediscovered by a few artists. Is it really a modern material? Is it not too strongly reminiscent of the admirable works of the past? How rare is the talent which can devote itself to such a tradition yet have nothing to fear from the inevitable comparisons! Still, our confidence is strengthened by these contemporary artists and their attempts to create new forms in their chosen material. For them, as for the ancients, bronze remains the symbol of the immortality of art.

Genuine or fake?

Techniques can be so perfected, and the experience accumulated in a traditional craft can become so great, that imitations of the highest quality become possible. Bronze founders in the artistic field do not use their skill and knowledge to deceive anybody – it is rather their customers who not infrequently do that! – but in order to render faithfully the forms handed down from the past. An attempt by Diego Giacometti has been made to rejuvenate certain aspects of the use of bronze in connection with furniture design.

Imitation need not find us completely helpless. For a start, we can appeal to our visual memory. If you are tempted to buy something, it is wise to analyse the feelings which attract you to it. Perhaps the object conveniently fills a gap in your decorative scheme; it is, let us say, the very chandelier you were looking for, or just the letter box required to put the finishing touch to your front door; in which case there is nothing more to be said. On the other hand, it may have given you that slight, but unmistakable, 'shock of recognition' which characterizes the presence of a work of art; and this brings us to the heart of the problem. What gave you this sense of recognition, what buried mechanism was activated by the object's appearance? Were you reminded of a similar object which you had seen illustrated in specialized journals or books, or admired in a museum or a friend's collection? Reflect a little; in some instances the resulting mental images will tell you that your response was engendered not by your instinct for a work of art but merely by memory and familiarity, just as in a crowd one sees a face one thinks one knows yet cannot be quite sure whether to speak or pass on. Sometimes the image will be sharp enough for you to identify it exactly. This is the moment at which to compare it with the object itself. Absence of the creative spirit is what shows up the fake. A faker *imitates*, he never innovates; if he did he would not be a faker. The most dangerous species of faker is no doubt the *pasticheur*, the man who is an adept at turning out an article 'in the manner of' some great master, but it should be remembered that, while a work of high quality is always harmonious and approaches perfection, pastiche is essentially the *accentuation of faults*. Most fakes are imitations of something well known, because it would not pay the faker to imitate anything else.

Until the end of the eighteenth century, bronze ornaments on furniture were always conceived as an integral part of the whole piece. But during the nineteenth century, decorative motifs became something applied to the piece; they were impeccable in execution, as before, but an army of nuts and bolts was necessary to fix them on. Every element had become a separate creation. Mechanical aids crept in, such as lathe turning and the grinding wheel. Whatever the work gained in the way of exactness and symmetry was more than offset by the loss of vitality and freedom. Nevertheless, bronze-workers continued to constitute an élite among craftsmen.

Is it a simple matter to tell modern work from antique? Yes, in our opinion; the difference consists not so much of skilful or clumsy workmanship as of higher or lower cost. Any bronze piece, fresh from the mould, is only a rough approximation to the finished article. It has yet to be worked up on the lathe, trimmed, chiselled and polished. But just how is this tool work done?

In the present day, accurate reproduction work, using the old methods, is perfectly feasible; there are craftsmen who, in work of the highest quality, employ the same techniques of chiselling and mercurial gilding as their predecessors. But commissions of this kind are exceptional; not many customers can afford them.

You would have to acquire first-hand knowledge of the

bronze-worker's tools to detect signs of them on the motifs: the chiselling, chasing and pearling, the beadings and delicate acanthus leaves and so on all have their own special tools, usually made by the craftsman himself to suit his own requirements.

Not having this knowledge of the craft, content yourself with examining all the bronze parts for traces of hand-tools and for any slight asymmetry. Tooling is in itself a sign of quality, even if the craftsman has abandoned his hand-tools in favour of mechanical aids. Conversely, distrust any bronze work in which the hollows and crannies have been left rough, as they came from the foundry, only the parts in relief and any smooth accessible surfaces having been polished, of course by machine; what you are looking at is undoubtedly an industrial product, mass-produced or thereabouts.

If possible, scrape the reverse side of one of the dubious bronze mounts. Examine the colour of the metal exposed and think of what is said in our section on 'Different kinds of bronze' to gauge the quality of the material.

Check on the patinas. Consult the chapter on 'Bronze and its patinas'; you will not take long to distinguish an artificial patina from a natural one.

Finally, there is the question of gilt bronze. Three techniques have been used. Mercurial gilding: this was the only method known to the ancient world; and no other was used before the end of the eighteenth century.

Mention should be made of *gold nitrate gilding*; and finally there is gilding by *electro-plating*, which employs electrolysis to cause molecular deposition. This method, used industrially, produces excellent results but, unlike mercurial gilding, makes it possible to deposit a very thin layer of gold, which will wear away sooner. To tell the difference between the two is a delicate matter, virtually impossible unless one has some means of gauging the thickness of the gilt. But there is this consolation, at any rate: gilded bronze means quality. We need hardly add that this applies only to art bronze; we are not referring to the vast output of anodized industrial products ranging from bathroom fittings to cocktail trolleys.

Different kinds of bronze

A knowledge of bronze and its states of conservation, enabling one both to judge it and to take care of it, will be acquired more easily if we examine some of the names and the numerous varieties of the alloy to which they are applied.

Bronze is an alloy of copper and tin. It properties are its low melting-point (1083 °C), suitability for casting, hardness, mechanical strength, sonority, brilliance when polished, and, above all, its colour, closely resembling gold. Bronze is made by adding tin to molten copper, the surface of the liquid metal in the crucible being protected by a layer of charcoal and a deoxidizer, usually cupro-phosphorus.

The proportion of copper to tin in the class of alloys known generally as 'bronze' has always been thoroughly haphazard, and is so still, in our opinion, where the manufacture of bronze for art is concerned. However, some attempt has been made to standardize the proportion in terms of the various uses for which the alloy is intended. Here is a brief review of these proportions.

For making medals and coins from flat sheet, 3–8 per cent of tin. These malleable bronzes are hard-wearing and keep their polish and colour well. They are also produced in bars (flats, squares, rounds, etc.) and wire, the latter being much used in jewellery.

8–12 per cent tin for machine parts, gears and anything exposed to sea water or certain other chemically aggressive media (some automobile parts, at least at one time; taps and other plumbing components, etc.). The Greeks and Romans made their bronze in this proportion.

13–20 per cent tin for high resistance to friction (bushes, bearings). Today, 83 per cent copper to 17 per cent tin is the ratio used for bronze destined for casting works of art.

20–30 per cent tin for casting bells and cymbals. Bronzes in this range have a low capacity for damping their own vibrations, hence their sonority.

30–40 per cent of tin is found in the bronze mirrors of antiquity. Bronzes in this range are hard, brittle and white. They polished exceptionally well and were thus highly suitable for their purpose.

Sixty seven per cent copper to 33 per cent tin is the ratio used at the present time for domestic purposes.

*

The colour of the bronzes mentioned so far varies according to the tin content and ranges from pink through greenish yellow to greyish white. The colour of any bronze object is a trustworthy criterion.

The composition of bronze displays a certain development down the centuries. As we have indicated, the amount of tin in bronze manufactured for a given purpose was far from constant; as time went on, moreover, other metals were added in an attempt to embody their special characteristics in the alloy and for cheapness.

An admixture of zinc, which is cheaper than either copper or tin, makes casting easier. Lead, similarly, makes the bronze easier to machine and also increases its plasticity, so that bronze containing from 5 to 30 per cent lead is used for moving parts in machinery. The same type of bronze also occurs fairly frequently in Roman coinage.

These bronzes containing tin and lead are those most commonly used because of their comparative cheapness and their suitability for machining. In theory, this range contains from 5 to 8 per cent tin, from 2 to 5 per cent zinc and from 1 to 5 per cent lead. But this classification is not very meaningful: when bronze of this type is used for a work of art, as is sometimes the case, the chief qualities aimed at are easy casting and a particular shade of colour.

Modern founders often use bronze provided by the scrap-metal industry, and I hope I shall not be accused of denigrating certain contemporary works of art if I point out that they owe a good deal to the plumbers who, by supplying old taps and gas-mantle burners for melting down, have made themselves very useful to the bronze founders. It is obviously impossible to specify the exact composition of the alloy produced.

To complete our review of the bronzes now in use, and the names of some of them, we mention:

'*Paris bronze*', an alloy of 88 per cent copper, 10 per cent zinc, 2 per cent lead. 'Bronze' is a misnomer in this case; the metal is brass with a little lead in it. Because of its pinkish golden colour and its working qualities it is used for making jewellery, ornaments and trinkets.

The quest for cheaper bronze resulted in alloys containing as much as 25 or 30 per cent zinc, during the last century and more particularly in the first part of this one. There must be a multitude of clocks, hanging lights and small sculptural figurines which were made of this metal and are still in good condition, despite the brittleness of the material.

For clock making, which demanded very delicate castings and complicated assemblies, the founders rejected orthodox bronze, preferring an alloy consisting of exactly 80 per cent copper, 4 per cent tin, 14 per cent zinc and 2 per cent lead; a compromise between bronze and brass.

White metal is used industrially for its low coefficient of friction; it consists mainly of tin, with small quantities of copper, antimony and lead. A similar alloy was used in large quantities during the early part of this century as an imitation bronze for manufacturing cheap ornaments.

This 'white metal', wrongly so called, was usually zinc thinly coated with bronze by means of galvanoplasty, or else a mixture of zinc and lead. The fracture of this alloy is characterized by the brilliance of the metallic crystalline structure. 'White metal' objects are usually regarded as worthless. But some antique dealers will have a 'white metal' article polished up, rendering it shiny and somewhat similar to pewter.

*

We end our survey with '*Zamac*', and escape from this tangle of genuine and spurious alloys through the back door, as it were; that is, by turning to the subject of fakes. '*Zamac*' was not developed by fakers but is frequently used as a substitute for bronze, despite resembling it neither in properties nor in appearance. It is an alloy of zinc and lead which casts easily, has about the same specific gravity as bronze, is cheap, readily accepts different patinas and is easier to carve or chase than genuine bronze. But why should the amateur concern himself with all this?

Simply to avoid being taken in. Some unscrupulous dealers, telling rather less than a half-truth, may offer to sell you pieces which they say are made of 'Zamac bronze' whereas the officially authorized name is 'zamac alloy'!

Bronze and its patinas

Patina is not, in itself, a guarantee that a supposed antique bronze is either old or genuine. Present-day bronze craftsmen claim to be able to reproduce any patina by chemical means. Collectors say it can't be done. Whom is one to believe?

In the section on 'Bronzes from excavations' we shall discuss what constitutes a patina and what does not, in cases where time and the atmosphere have wreaked some degree of destruction. Here we shall glance briefly at bronze in its normal states of maturity.

Velvet black

This patina is specially typical of Far Eastern bronzes. As its name indicates, it is a fairly deep black; sometimes it has a bottle-green sheen. The finest velvety patinas of all are said to be produced by stroking with the human hand.

Green

Bronze from the ancient world (see 'Bronzes from excavations') exhibit many different shades of green, particularly blue-greens. All are caused by copper oxide mingled with extraneous substances.

'Embugadon'

This name is applied to a reddish-brown patina common to many Eastern and Far Eastern pieces (including Indian): sometimes it is as deep in colour as wine-lees.

Medallion black

Fairly dark, with glints of brown; almost matt; perfectly smooth; found on medals and on Egyptian bronze figurines.

Renaissance rose

Sixteenth-century bronzes have a very beautiful patina, usually brown, but on the parts in relief the metal shows through – a very characteristic pinkish-yellow ground (typical of Florentine bronzes).

Domestic articles of the sixteenth and seventeenth centuries exhibit various patinas, many of which recall the 'black velvet' patina of Far Eastern bronzes on a ground of light yellow with a cool gleam.

Obviously all these different shades, named or unnamed, depend on appreciation; they are subjective. In most cases they are the direct outcome of the composition of the alloy, the treatment to which it has been subjected and in some cases the use to which the article has been put, and the substances with which it has come into contact.

'Artificial' patinas

Workshop secrets for the treatment of bronze abound, according to traditional craftsmen. They may or may not be right.

Bronze having formed part of industrial manufacture for the last one hundred and fifty years at least, it must be difficult to shroud any of the stock techniques in secrecy. Certainly every craftsman may have his own special skills, or a favourite chemical recipe – probably not much different from the next man's – but that is as far as it goes.

Bain de Barèges or pierre de Barèges

It is not exactly known what this substance, *pierre de Barèges*, 'Barèges stone', owes to the Pyrenean spa from which it takes its name; probably something to do with the sulphur in the waters. In any case, 'Barèges stone' is a colouring matter which forms the basis for several patinas. The bronze is first thoroughly cleaned, preferably with mild acid (such as vinegar), coated with a special varnish or with 'ageing' oil and rubbed with *pierre de Barèges*, which is available in various suitable colours for use on bronze.

Polish

The piece to be treated is strongly heated and then given a coat of ordinary wax. The liquid constituents of the wax evaporate and the colouring matter is left on the metal. After drying, the piece is rubbed with a cloth to shine it up and brighten the parts in relief.

A 'natural' patina

This much-used method gives a fairly natural-looking patina. The piece is well heated and plunged into clean mineral oil. The bronze instantaneously loses the brand-new appearance which it inevitably possesses as it comes from the craftsman's hand, and acquires a warm colour.

'Antique' green

This can be produced with *pierre de Barèges*; another way is to use sulphuric acid, somewhat diluted. The resulting oxidation can be fixed with varnish or beeswax.

The most convincing 'antique' green of all which anyone can use with the cooperation of an obliging chemist or drugstore is to add to 100 grammes of acetic acid, 10 grammes of ammonium carbonate, 10 grammes of bay salt, 10 grammes of potassium tartrate diluted with a little water. Coat the bronze with this mixture and leave it exposed to the air for two or three days, by the end of which time it will have turned a beautiful green. Tidy up the oxidations with a brush and apply a coat of wax.

Deep black

Here is a common device which works like a charm on bronze furniture mounts that look glaringly new. A quick dip in ammonia gives them a blue-black gleam. Ammonium carbonate blackens them completely. All you have to do is to complete the patina with a little wax, or a mixture of Sienese earth and turpentine, and polish up the articles slightly so as to emphasize the relief.

The care of antique bronze

The patina of a bronze must be respected, there can be no argument about that; one should never reduce bronze to the brilliance of well-polished copper or brass. It is generally agreed that bronze should retain the imprint of time which adds to its character.

A bronze in good condition can be cleaned with soapy water and a soft brush which will penetrate the detail. After rinsing it should be dried in dry air (on a central-heating radiator or an electric radiator), then hot-waxed with melted beeswax. When the work has cooled completely, remove excess wax with a brush and rub with a woollen duster.

The care of bronze mounts on furniture

Bronze on genuine antique furniture has in most cases been gilded. Metal polish would merely have the effect of wearing the gilding away and eventually eliminating it. At first this appears not to be so, because the brightness of the bronze looks like gilding, but in the long run the discoloration of the metal will draw attention to the difference. Admittedly the gilding will be worn away only on the raised parts and will remain intact between them: on the other hand, the accumulated residues of polish, wax and dust in the hollows will prevent the gilding from being seen.

First stage: cleaning

A soft brush (preferably of vegetable fibres) and some soapy water to which a little detergent has been added will enable you to get rid of the encrusted deposits which have accumulated in the details of the bronze motifs. Persevere until everything is completely clean. You can then see at once whether any gilding is left. Gold does not corrode and is therefore bound to regain its brightness directly it is cleaned. Rinse and dry the parts you have washed. To prevent water from running over the rest of the piece, keep a sponge handy or protect the surface with a sheet of plastic held down by adhesive tape.

If any gilding is left

Bring your bronzes back to their original state of polish by rubbing with a chamois leather. Don't use a polishing paste; it contains abrasives. At most, use tripoli or some similar harmless powder, applying it dry and working with a light hand; then dust the motifs with a soft brush.

If no gilding is left

This gives you a free hand; you can't damage what isn't there.

Thoroughly clean the bronze parts and then shine them up with any of the established metal polishes used for brass. But at all costs avoid accumulations of polish in the crannies; when drying out they turn white. So remove them with a brush before shining up.

A few time-savers

On clean bronze, whether gilded or not, apply a 1:1 dilution of nitric acid. The metal shines immediately. Rinse, and rub with a soft cloth or a chamois leather.

Another mixture which is slightly more complicated but giving excellent results is 20 grammes of nitric acid in 80 grammes of water, with the addition of a little aluminium sulphate.

Cabinet makers pressed for time use concentrated nitric acid to which they add a little salt and a little lamp-black.

Whenever possible, bronze mounts should be removed before cleaning; most of the preparations used for cleaning or stripping them are harmful to wood or varnish.

The preparations mentioned here work most efficiently if the items to be cleaned are first heated to about 100 °C.

To remove the mounts you can pull out the nails with a pair of pliers or pincers, using a piece of cardboard as a template to avoid marking the bronze or the wood. Sometimes the mounts are fixed by screws, in which case use a screwdriver of the right size.

Once clean and shiny again, the mounts can be protected against tarnishing by means of a clear varnish.

Bronze sculpture and its editions

Bronze sculptures attract the collector: a profusion of forms and styles, *plus* famous signatures and the interest of the different 'editions'. Demand is continually rising for short runs (small editions) dating from the late nineteenth or early twentieth century, particularly of the works of Rodin, Pradier and Maillol and of the animal sculptors such as Barye, Rosa and Isidore Bonheur, Pompon, P.-J. Mène and others.

This increased demand obviously invites forgeries, especially as most of the works concerned are old enough to be no longer subject to copyright. There is, however, one peculiarity which reveals the fakes. The faker naturally needs a genuine work from which to make his copy; this is called *surmoulage* (there seems to be no specifically corresponding term in English). In principle this ought to yield a perfect replica, but in practice there is always a definite though varying degree of shrinkage; we can take it as being about 10 per cent of the original volume. There are several reasons for this, the main one being the expansion of the molten metal and perhaps of the mould as well. Another is that the original went through the normal finishing process, it was tooled and polished; the same will apply to the replica and this means a further reduction in size.

So be careful when buying a numbered bronze. Demand a certificate of genuineness or consult a specialist, unless you are absolutely sure about size and, moreover, are familiar with the dimensions of the original.

On the first edition it is usual to find a second signature. This is the founder's stamp; examples are Hébrard for the bronzes of Daumier, Barbedienne for some (but not all) of those of Barye, Mène, Fratin, etc.

This second signature, though not an absolute guarantee, is a valuable indication.

This is a field in which the French, as in the making of ormolu, have established complete ascendancy over the English, as a comparison of the following list of names will show: John Willis Good, Lord Leighton, Charles Ricketts, Alfred Stevens. Set these names against those of Rodin, Maillol and Pradier, and the palm must be conceded. Only John Macallan Swan can be set alongside the French artists as a true *animalier*, and he was taught all he knew by Frémiet.

Bronzes from excavations

Bronzes from excavations, whether Oriental, Greek, Roman, Etruscan or Gaulish, are usually small objects which time and conditions underground have attacked in a greater or lesser degree; we hasten to add that bronze is highly resistant to deterioration of various kinds. After an initial phase of surface oxidation a buried object becomes stabilized; deterioration slows down. The oxides cause chemical reactions in the surrounding soil and mineralize it. The real danger comes when the object is disturbed. The chlorides that have eaten into the bronze will then absorb water vapour from the atmosphere, and ignorance of the real nature and treatment can result in nothing being left on the shelf of a display case but a mound of green dust, a derisory monument to an object now defunct.

The danger of oak

Roman money was subject to frequent devaluation: sometimes coins were minted in more or less base metals, and there was a whole numismatic period, about 500 B.C., when currency was manufactured from lead bronze. Not all collectors are able to house their treasures in cabinets lined with plush or velvet; sometimes they use an ordinary cupboard – not realizing that an oak drawer may be fatal. Oak, in fact, gives off acetic acid which combines with lead and transforms it into a carbonate. The first symptom of this chemical attack is the presence of a greyish dust on the surface of the object. Don't wait for further developments, re-house your collection.

Egyptian bronzes

It is hard to lay down general rules for these figurines and other objects; the alloys are pretty haphazard and some are short of tin, which was very scarce in ancient Egypt. Most contain lead. The dry, hot climate of the banks of the Nile has had a strong preservative effect on the pieces that have come down to us, and the Cairo Museum has the reputation of providing the most salubrious environment in the world. But the oxidation of bronze, and in particular the agglomerations of copper salts on the surface of the object, have picked up silica in varying amounts. There is general agreement today that Egyptian bronzes should be cleaned and the original colour of the metal brought to light.

There is an important question of principle here: ought the oxidations coating the majority of excavated bronzes to be removed or not? For many years the green colour produced by copper salts was like a signature authenticating ancient bronzes. Today the preference is to restore the object to its original appearance. There are two arguments to suggest that this course is not arbitrary. Careful cleaning has often revealed details (chisellings, encrusted decoration, gilt and even inscriptions) which would have remained hidden under the layer of mineralized oxides.

Again, it is dangerous not to know what reactions are going on beneath that layer; whereas if the object is clean it is easy enough to tell whether the surface is active or not. A covering of alien substances might delay detection until too late.

Bronzes from Greece, Rome, Gaul and elsewhere

A good quality of alloy was used for many of these, the tin content being the very correct one of from 8 to 15 per cent. Their state depends on age and the conditions surrounding them at the time of discovery. Don't hesitate to clean them; real concretions are very hard and only those foreign bodies which are loosely attached will come off, a desirable result from every point of view. The contemporary doctrine on conservation is to remove everything which is 'exterior' to the form. Just what does this mean?

An object from an excavation has undergone molecular changes; oxidation is not just a superficial phenomenon but coincides with zones of weakness in the metal, microscopic fissures. The copper salts colonize their environment and eventually effect a mineralization which engenders stable substances: nitrates and carbonates such as malachite and azurite. This mineralization is, by definition, *exterior*, at least as regards its visible part. It is the proof of the genuineness of the object; some of it, therefore, should be left undisturbed provided it does not ruin some line or volume of an object.

These indications are a guide in exposing fakes. No fabricated 'patina', no deterioration artificially contrived with acids or other chemicals is capable of marking the very substance of which the faked piece is made. Experts are well aware of this and can test the genuineness of the piece merely by passing a hand over it.

How to clean bronzes from excavations

We must advise moderation. Anything which might damage an object or diminish the signs of its authenticity must be rigorously avoided. On the other hand an ancient bronze, if it is to be preserved at all, does require a certain amount of treatment. In prescribing it, we must adhere consistently to the principles and methods we have assembled for your benefit.

An object still covered with soil, etc., should be gently brushed.

When its general outlines emerge use a scalpel to loosen identifiable extraneous substances.

Provided you can see nothing abnormal – notably a tendency on the part of the object and the matter clinging to it to come away in pulverized form – wash the bronze in a bath whose composition must be *strictly* as follows:

To every ½ litre of water: 90 grammes of sodium or potassium tartrate; 30 grammes of caustic soda; and a little hydrogen peroxide (see page 6).

Any chemist or drugstore can provide the ingredients.

Place the object in the mixture. Try a little of the mixture on part of the object first. After ten minutes, take the object out and examine the effect. In theory, all foreign bodies should have dissolved except the mineralized accumulations. Help things along by brushing. If nothing has happened, reimmerse the object for another thirty minutes or, at the most, one hour. If you notice any change in the colour on the part of the object, particularly a reddish tinge, take the object out and rinse it, then place it in water to which 5 per cent of sulphuric acid has been added. This completes the washing process, though you can supplement it with a rinse in a mineral water of high purity, such as Evian, which may dissolve any chlorides remaining in the fissures of the surface. At this stage in the cleaning it is essential to check whether these chlorides are present or not, because the accelerated oxidation observed in objects from excavations depends on the presence or absence of chlorides in their molecules. How are you to tell whether there are any chlorides there and, if so, how do you get rid of them?

Concealed chlorides

Facilities exist in specialized museums for making scientific analyses to detect and chemically identify these chlorides. This is something you can't do, and it doesn't matter.

You should follow the restorers employed by the museums.

After washing the object get it absolutely dry. In doing so, *never* heat it above 100–120 °C; at any higher temperature expansion would produce new microscopic cracks and open the door to further chemical attack. Use an infra-red lamp, an electric fire or a hair drier or any other source of *dry heat*, free of noxious combustion products like those of gas.

Improvise a 'damp chamber' which can be tightly closed; place some water in it and suspend the object to be tested above the water level. The humidity will soon show up in chlorides which become visible in a few hours. You can recognize their presence by droplets of water on the surface of the object, characteristic tiny globules, slightly cloudy, sometimes with a 'skin' on them, like blisters on the patina. If dried with blotting paper, they will re-form in a few hours.

It is an excellent omen if the phenomenon is only slight: a small amount of chlorides is easy to neutralize, as we shall shortly show. If, on the other hand, the drops are prominent, special treatment will be necessary and highly complicated processes exist for eliminating chlorides by ultrasonics. *The effectiveness of the process suggested here is equalled only by its simplicity.*

Prepare a mixture by dissolving some gelatine in 1 litre of water at boiling point; add 2–3 grammes of agar-agar and 6–10 grammes of glycerine.

Cover the object with the mixture as thickly as possible; the coating should be 2 or 3 mm deep. Wrap it in thin aluminium foil, place the parcel in the damp chamber and leave it. After a few hours you will see that the aluminium is being corroded; it will have a hole in it somewhere, or several holes. Wash the wrapping – with the object still inside – being specially thorough at and round the holes; add little more of the gelatine mixture and cover the holes with pieces of foil.

Continue the process until the foil wrapping is used up; you can then thoroughly clean the object, apply another coat of the mixture and put on a new wrapping.

When all the chlorides have been drawn from the bronze to attack the aluminium, you will see that the 'blisters' which previously disfigured the object have disappeared, leaving a clean surface. Finish off with thorough rinsing, followed by brushing and drying.

Preservation of bronzes

Do not let the object cool after drying; it would absorb humidity. Dip it in melted wax (60 °C), a mixture of natural beeswax and 5 per cent of carnauba wax (a very hard vegetable wax with the comparatively high melting point of 110–120 °C, which can be obtained from specialized firms which deal with cabinet makers. It is worth noting that some high-quality furniture polishes contain carnauba wax).

When the object has cooled and the wax has set, just polish it up with a soft cloth. The same very simple method is applicable to bronzes in good condition or only slightly affected. It has the advantage of neutralizing the chlorides by isolating them from the humidity of the atmosphere. But take the precaution of adding a fungicide to the wax (a few drops of formaldehyde, for example), to protect it from the possibility of attack by microorganisms.

Another method, and special cases

An object which is actively crumbling, becoming powdery, must not be subjected to washing, which would probably be fatal. If certain factors have caused the tin in the alloy to become dissociated, the only possible course is to consolidate the surface by impregnating it with cellulose varnish. The first coat should be heavily diluted (five or ten times more solvent than varnish), the others less so. If possible, apply the varnish by dipping.

Can bronzes be repaired?

This is too specialized a question for us to deal with it at length. Every case must be studied separately. However, plastic resins have now opened up huge possibilities especially as some of these resins can be coloured so accurately as to merge perfectly with the whole.

Bronzes from excavations

The greater wealth of metallic objects brought to light by archaeology is now seen in museums all over the country.

To restore all the objects deposited in these museums would

take thousands of years. But it is thought that an object which has survived fifteen hundred years underground may totally disintegrate in fifty or a hundred years when exposed on a shelf in a display case.

4 Carpets and tapestries

Carpets and tapestries

Carpets and tapestries are made by different techniques, but in dealing with the two in a single chapter we are not perpetrating a confusion of *genres*. Briefly, the difference is that a carpet is composed of knots attached to a warp, whereas a tapestry is needlework carried out in a frame.

What we wish to emphasize is the obvious connection between them. There are excellent grounds for supposing they had a common origin. It cannot be seriously denied that the chief creators of both were the nomadic peoples whose seasonal migrations ranged between the Eastern Mediterranean lands and the steppes of the Far East. To this very day there are nomadic tribes living in the old way, moving from pasture to pasture, whose rugs and carpets are the most sought after by the collector.

As for the difference between carpets and tapestries, it is certainly not one of function. In a nomad's tent, a carpet is not used solely for covering the ground; it may also be mural decoration, partition or couch-cover. Equally, the celebrated French 'carpets' from the Savonnerie are, in many cases, handworked on a loom.

The vogue for carpets and tapestries in the West began with the return of the crusaders. Up to the sixteenth century, architecture was mainly military in conception and built for strength rather than comfort. For monarchs of the time, carpets and tapestries were a necessity and not a luxury. They made it possible to create smaller rooms within the damp great hall of a fortified castle and to mask the cold unsightly roughness of the walls. The Emperor Charles had his collection always with him, whether at Aix, Ghent, or Madrid.

Renaissance architecture, though more appealing than that of the feudal period, was equally remote from the human scale; and the Château of Chambord, on a tributary of the Loire, may have been even chillier than Château-Gaillard, towering above the Seine; carpets and tapestries were necessary as well as ornamental.

A sign of the directly utilitarian aspect of tapestry in the Middle Ages, and even after the Renaissance, is its almost unchanging technique. From its thirteenth-century beginnings until the sixteenth century, only about fifty colours were used.

Apart from the introduction of gold and silver thread there were no innovations before the late seventeenth century, by which time 10,000 different shades of colour had come into use.

Carpets, on the other hand, were something special and apart. They came from the Middle East and, being expensive, were precious. They were rarely used as floor-coverings, coarse mats were good enough for that; historians tell us that the flagstones in castle interiors were often covered with straw. Doubtless it was only in a few of the least primitive, rustic rooms that carpets were used for their original purpose.

Nevertheless in paintings of interior scenes, prior to the seventeenth century, carpets are in evidence mainly as tablecloths and sometimes on ceremonial daïses. Such details are common in pictures signed by Holbein, Le Nain, Vermeer, Pieter de Hooch, Gabriel Metzu and Abraham Bosse.

Henri IV of France tried to make carpets after the fashion of Turkey and the Levant available to his people by setting up workshops. The industry had since prospered and been mechanized, but the machine-made carpet, though within reach of most pockets, remains devoid of charm. There is no substitute.

In 1844 the novelist George Sand, during a visit to the Château de Boussac in the valley of the River Creuse, discovered the sumptuous six-piece series representing *The Lady and the Unicorn*.

Her enthusiasm was such that she converted her contemporaries to a taste for medieval tapestries which saved many masterpieces from oblivion.

Buying a carpet

Suppose you have picked out a carpet which suits your taste, the the use for which you intend it, and your pocket. You have made sure it is a genuine knotted carpet, not a machine-made one (see below). What else should you look for? Hold it up against the light from a window, and look at it from the back. Weak places, holes and repairs will show up at once.

A carpet of high quality should be soft and supple. This can be checked first by the feel of it in your hand, then by letting it fall on to itself in a crumpled heap. There should be no stiffness anywhere.

Also examine it carefully for rot in the fibres. You can sometimes spot it by the colour having altered or faded, but not always. It is a serious fault, caused by prolonged exposure to damp, whether in a warehouse, the hold of a ship or an empty house. All you have to do is to examine the warp for soundness by pulling it firmly in various directions and at different places. Rub the carpet between your hands like a washerwoman, then stretch it boldly. A faint but characteristic rending sound will inform you of its condition.

Knots, abrachs, dates

Knots

It is a difficult task for an amateur to identify the type of knot from a superficial examination. However, the sketches given here are a guide. The vital thing is to be able to tell at a glance whether a carpet was made by hand or machine, as this considerably affects its value.

There are *two* main types of knot: the Ghiordes or Turkish, and the Senne (Sehna, Senneh) or Persian.

The *Ghiordes knot* encircles two strands of the warp; its ends come out between them and constitute the pile.

The *Senne knot* goes round only one strand of the warp; one end comes out next to that strand, the other passes under the adjacent strand and comes out without having gone round it.

If the Senne knot goes round both strands it is a sign that the carpet is incorrectly made, possibly even a fake, although produced by hand.

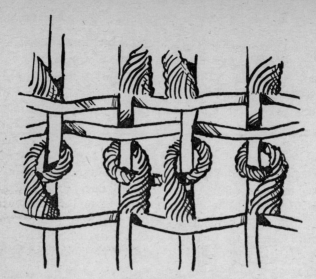

Ghiordes knot

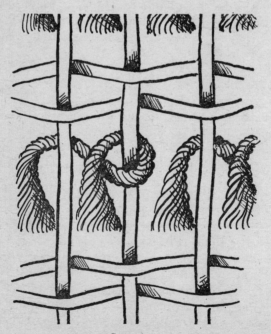

Senne knot

The *'double' knot* (*tête d'alouette*, 'lark's head') is a sign of Western handicraft, in which the warp is in reality a canvas (like an embroidery canvas).

Industrially manufactured carpets are easy to identify: there are no knots. The 'pile' is not really a pile at all, but a velvet whose fibres are held in place only by the tension of the weaving. A simple little test is enough to demonstrate this: isolate a single fibre, and pull. It will come away easily.

Abrachs: defect or merit?

A really old carpet may display variations in colour, particularly in the background. You will sometimes see different shades of red, blue or some other colour. These details, which stand out most prominently when they occur in prominent parts of the pattern, are called *abrachs*. It should be remembered that making a carpet is a long-term job and that, under the conditions of nomadic life, wool is prepared as and when wanted. The colours are usually natural vegetable or mineral dyes. They are fast to light, excellently so, but vary in shade because the ingredients may have been mixed in varying proportions, and because the water available in one place, as the tribe seasonally migrates, may differ from that in another. The *abrachs* are irregular contrasts which give an indispensable liveliness to the whole. Work produced in factories established by royal decree is almost always devoid of *abrachs*, which are essentially defects; but we must point out that the presence of these has never detracted from the value of a fine carpet; indeed, they may be part of its charm.

Dates

Determining when a carpet was made is a matter for specialists. Apart from a few exceptional pieces which can safely be said to be several centuries old, most antique carpets are a hundred years old at the outside. We must remember that in most cases we are dealing with a folk art, in which the relevant criterion is not so much age as spontaneity. Dating a carpet therefore does not matter much, except for information and interest. But, with this reservation in mind, it is worth knowing the system of the Islamic calendar. It begins at the Hegira, the day on which Mahomet fled from Mecca; in our terms 16 July A.D. 622.

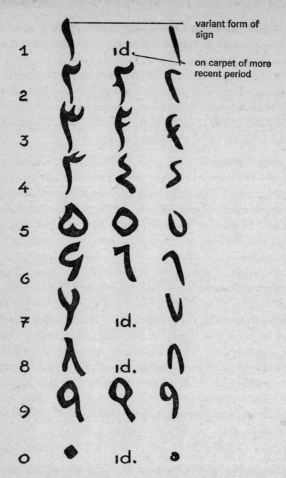

1		id.	variant form of sign
			on carpet of more recent period
2			
3			
4			
5			
6			
7		id.	
8		id.	
9			
0		id.	

Oriental numbers indicating date of manufacture of carpet. The first two columns give the old forms of the numbers; the third column, those found on carpets of recent manufacture

The Islamic year is several days shorter than ours; thirty-two of our years correspond to thirty-three of theirs. By means of some simple arithmetic any Islamic date can be expressed in our own chronology. Divide the date on the carpet by thirty-three; subtract the quotient from the dividend and add the 622 years from the start of the Hegira.

For example:

Islamic date   1221
divided by 33:   37
$1221 - 37 = 1184$
$1184 + 622 = 1806,$
the date according to the Gregorian calendar.

The date of manufacture is sometimes on the edge of the carpet, close to a corner; sometimes close to the central motif. In more recent pieces it is written on a piece of cloth sewn on to the back of the carpet, and the place of manufacture is also given.

Our numerical symbols, though known as 'Arabic figures', have lost almost all resemblance to their distant ancestors. The present-day Eastern forms, moreover, display local variations.

Distortions

The fact that a carpet was made by hand, on a warp stretched on a fairly primitive loom, and also the fact that some of its fibres will since have shrunk, will have caused it to have been pulled out of shape to some degree. These distortions are often a sign of genuineness but sometimes make the carpet wear in an uneven, unsightly way. A badly distorted carpet must be given a flexible backing which will prevent the members of the warp from shifting this way or that. Thick flannel or felt, or plastic foam sheet, is the answer.

Borders: always keep a sharp eye on the state of a carpet's edges. Neglect often allows damage to begin developing. The sides of a carpet are reinforced simply by closely set whipstitching. You don't need to be an expert with the needle to repair and maintain the edges of a carpet; there is nothing difficult about it (see diagram of whipstitching).

Fringes: these get worn out and may even disappear completely. This is very serious; a fringe is composed of the ends of the warp, and when it wears away the whole carpet may begin coming to pieces. Action is urgently required. As a general rule it is better to go to a professional and get him to reconstitute the threatened part. If you think the carpet is not worth the expense you can try yourself.

All the strands of the warp must be caught and 'stopped' with chainstitch, possibly with several parallel rows of chainstitch. But take care to avoid extremes: the stitches must neither be drawn too tight, which would crimp the edge of the carpet, nor left too loose, which would serve no purpose, giving too little support to the warp.

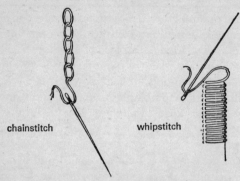

chainstitch   whipstitch

Afterwards you can buy some worsted or cotton fringe, which is sold by the yard in shops specializing in such things, and sew it on in place of the original fringe.

The importance of this artificial fringe is obviously not only aesthetic, it prevents wear.

Cleaning

Nothing in a house or flat is so much exposed to dust and dirt as a carpet. Its pile has the further unfortunate privilege of attracting its own deadliest enemies: clothes-moths and their eggs and larvae. Careful maintenance can contribute directly to the preservation of a carpet, but it must also be remembered that violent or incompetent cleaning can do more harm than the worst depredations by parasites.

The vacuum cleaner is perfect for daily use; but *don't*, please, use the head which has a hard brush, it would inflict an excessive amount of wear. And don't shake the carpet out of the window; the carpet's whole weight is borne by the small portion of the warp gripped by your hands, and every shake, whether violent or gentle, adds to the strain.

Slinging the carpet over a line and beating it is also a treatment to be avoided, or at any rate, to use only in moderation. Don't give great hefty blows but light, quick taps; and don't do it more than twice a year. Mechanical carpet-beaters with brushes mounted on rollers are not advisable either.

The vacuum cleaner, of course, only keeps the surface of the carpet clean; the dust goes much deeper, becoming encrusted in the pile and warp. Only large, specialized firms, with the necessary equipment, can deep-clean your carpet.

In the long run, despite care, your carpet will lose its brilliance; the light colours will be dim, the dark ones dusty.

If only superficial cleaning is required buy one of the carpet shampoos available. They work well and do not necessarily involve moving the carpet first, being usable almost dry. A damp sponge after shampooing is all that is required; no messy rinsing. The result will be good as far as it goes, but will be no more than a visual effect; the deep-lying dirt will not be affected. A similar effect can be obtained with a soft brush dipped into a mixture of ammonia and water (2 parts water, 1 part ammonia); follow this by brushing with water to which a little vinegar has been added.

Disasters great and small

There is no end to these, alas! Cigarette burns in the pile are the worst. Fortunately wool is not highly combustible and the damage never spreads far. Repair consists of surrounding the hole with one or more rings of stitching on the back of the carpet so as to strengthen the warp, and then, if necessary, rebuilding the warp by stitching criss-cross – darning, in fact. Finally, to show your dexterity by building up the missing bit of pattern, knot pieces of wool round the warp you have renewed, and cut them off exactly flush with embroidery scissors.

Chewing gum sticks the pile together, which gets trodden flat and looks hideous, and is luckily not as hard to remove as it might seem. Never try to prise it off with a knife or any other tool. Take a clean rag, wet it with acetone and rub gently. The gum will soon dissolve.

Grease-spots: talc or Fuller's earth will help you get grease out of a carpet. Dust it on the affected part of the pile, leave it for twenty-four hours, and brush it off thoroughly. If the spot is still there, wet it with benzene, first placing an absorbent rag under the carpet. On a very light-coloured carpet (this applies specially to Chinese carpets) use ether instead of benzene; it cuts the grease without leaving a halo. But you will do well to proceed cautiously with little dabs, not letting the solvent run far.

Ink is dreadful! If you get there in time, boldly swab the spot with a wet sponge, taking care not to spread the stain further; then hold it under a cold tap to dilute the remaining ink as much as possible; if necessary, turn the tap off at intervals, swab off the water, then repeat. This will avert the worst damage.

If the stain has already dried, consult a specialist. All treatments powerful enough to deal with an inkstain are harmful to carpets; only a specialist has the necessary remedies and precautions at his command.

Urine: carpets are liable to being wetted with urine, which is usually corrosive to some degree, by pets and small children. Never regard this lightly; swab the place at once, otherwise the colours, and perhaps the warp and the knots, will suffer. Proceed as for ink. Make sure the affected place has dried out completely before putting the carpet back.

Insects: even the best-kept houses are not immune from predators which sometimes are tiny or even invisible. Those which are specifically dangerous to carpets include moths, carpet beetles (fortunately rare in our temperate climate) and mites. Insecticides which deal with these have long been known, notably the familiar naphthalene, and others based on benzene and chlorine; but their smell makes them unacceptable in a drawing-room, living-room or bedroom. Aerosols and DDT powder work well, except that they do not affect the insects' eggs. Perhaps the young larvae will be killed; not necessarily, however, without having had time to attack a few essential fibres before ingesting the poison. However, there is a simple means of ensuring that any living eggs in a carpet get killed off: refrigeration. If you have a large enough refrigerator, treat your carpet to as long a stay in it as possible (not less than forty-eight hours), and let the carpet be close to the freezer. If the fridge is too small send the carpet to a specialized firm which has large refrigerating chambers.

Exposing the carpet to frost in winter, provided the air is dry, will do no harm – and no good, because it is in the spring and summer that moths, etc., are most active.

Where and how to lay a carpet

A few precautions – elementary, no doubt, yet requiring mention. Anyone can see that the feet of chairs and other furniture, stiletto heels, or much going to and fro, can subject a carpet to abnormal wear. When laying a carpet, avoid the 'main road' through a room; don't put the carpet under furniture; and do put felt pads on the feet of chairs. An uneven floor is the worst enemy of the warp of a carpet – loose parquet blocks, rough or badly laid tiles. Always protect a carpet with an under felt or a thin sheet of flexible foam plastic.

Do your carpet justice

Notice that every carpet has a direction, a 'grain' as it were. The pattern itself usually makes this clear; in any case the shimmer of the colours will do so. The pile, in fact, always points in the direction of the knotting and absorbs or reflects the light accordingly. When laying it, take care to choose the position most favourable to its beauty. Similarly, when buying a carpet examine it from various angles to make sure how it really looks.

Hanging a tapestry

The way in which a tapestry is hung determines whether it remains in a good state of preservation or not. There are two schools of thought about this.

One maintains that a tapestry must be kept supple and that it was always intended to be allowed a certain amount of movement. The other school argues that a tapestry should hang against a wall as it did on the loom, i.e. stretched tight, with every detail of the design plain to see.

There is a logical solution; namely to hang the tapestry so that it is taut along the top, while the sides, bottom and surface in general are left loose.

An important point is that a tapestry should never be in contact with a wall, however sound. Old tapestries, regrettably, display marks left by damp.

Orientation

Textiles in general, particularly if coloured, are endangered by sunlight. It is claimed for the old natural dyes, both vegetable and mineral, that they are fast to light. This is true but not absolutely so. On the other hand, it is noticeable that certain colours have resisted the ravages of time and ill-treatment. The set of tapestries of the Apocalypse, which are now the favourite child of the National Fine Arts Administration in France and have been given a remarkable museum all to themselves in the castle of King René at Angers, were once used as horse-blankets and coverings for vegetable frames on the episcopal estate in that locality! Though undoubtedly no longer as fresh as when completed, five centuries ago, they are still admirable.

Tapestries, then, should not be hung opposite sunny windows. Even oblique sunlight is to be avoided. Hang a tapestry on a section of wall between two windows, out of reach of the sun. Give it suitable artificial lighting if need be, but do not let the bulbs be too near it; their heat would dehydrate the fibres excessively and cause local fading.

Secure suspension

To keep the tapestry away from the wall, fix to the wall a square-section wooden batten which can be anything from 3–6 cm thick; this will provide the necessary separation and an adequate surface for suspension. A tapestry can't be just pinned up like a poster. The damage done by that method can easily be seen in old tapestries, which are stretched out of shape and disfigured by holes, indelible rust-stains, etc. Various other methods are available to you which are not only kinder to the tapestry than using nails but have the additional advantage of making it easily removable.

Rings

A simple solution is to sew curtain-rings on to the back of the tapestry and to hang it on a curtain-rod or hooks. To keep these arrangements out of sight, sew the rings on 5–7 cm below the edge. The edges of the tapestry should always be strengthened with stout braid, which should be as wide as possible.

'Flemish' curtain-hooks
This type of curtain-hook is designed for double curtains. Sew them to the braid at intervals of about 25 cm. The advantage of 'Flemish' hooks is that they cannot be seen and that they make it easier to conceal the rod.

The best solution of all
Border the back of the tapestry with 'Velcro' right across the top (and down the sides too, if you like), The corresponding strip of 'Velcro' is fastened, either with hooks or an adhesive, to the wooden strip. This is the solution we regard as the best in every way. We have found by experience that 'Velcro' is quite strong enough and holds securely, in addition to enabling one to stretch the tapestry evenly.

Looking after tapestries
In writing of carpets and how to clean them, we looked in detail at various products and the ways in which they could be used in special cases. Most of them are also perfectly suitable for tapestries.

But there are also special problems posed by tapestries, demanding specific answers.

Beware of insects! Moths and silver-fish are even deadlier enemies of tapestries than of carpets. A tapestry hung on a wall is easy to treat with an insecticide in powder form. Or you can sew little bags on to the back and fill them with paradichlorbenzene.

If you see any silver-fish on the tapestry you should realize at once that it is threatened by a more insidious enemy than these insects themselves, which can be killed immediately with a good insecticide. Silver-fish need a high degree of humidity in order to live, and their presence is a warning sign that your tapestry is suffering from damp. Either move it elsewhere or damp-proof the wall.

Cleaning is based on the application of ox-gall, a natural substance which not only removes dirt but brightens the colours. Dry shampoos containing ox-gall, for carpets and tapestries, are easy to buy. Diluted with water, they produce abundant froth, which is what you use. Pick it up on a very soft brush and apply a moderate amount all over the surface; assist its action by brushing, preferably parallel to the weave. Make a pad of a clean white rag which doesn't fray, and remove the froth with it; whenever the pad gets dirty, re-fold it so as always to work with a clean part. Continue wiping until the pad ceases to pick up dirt.

You can finish off by lightly wiping with a rag dipped in water with a little vinegar in it; squeeze the rag out well after each dip.

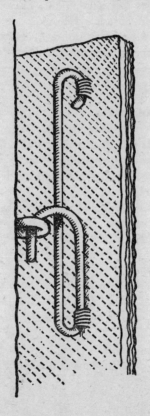

5 Chairs

Learn to re-seat chairs

You possess some well-made cottage chairs whose straw is in an advanced stage of disrepair and beginning to show ominous, ugly gaps. What is to be done – short of discovering a forgotten craftsman in a backyard or a rustic hovel? The answer is simple: do it yourself.

The difficulty, despite your good intentions, is where to find the straw. It must be the right kind, rye straw. But rye is rarely grown today. The only thing is to scour the countryside, asking farmers where to get this indispensable material. Without it, good results are impossible: oat straw is too short, wheat straw too brittle. If your search proves in vain, try a manufacturer who specializes in cottage furniture; you can probably find one who won't begrudge you a truss or so of rye straw. Moreover, it will have the advantage of being already dyed and treated against attack by mice. The usual amount to allow is 250 grammes per chair.

If you have bought your straw straight from the farm you can either use it with its natural colour intact, or give it a goldish hue by the following means: fill a preserving pan or similar vessel with water; cut the straw at the knots and lay it in the water, all pointing the same way. Bring the water to the boil and let it simmer a whole day. Leave it to cool overnight. Then take out the straw and spread it to dry thoroughly before use.

As well as the stout rye straw you may need the long, thin blades of various plants or grasses. This can be used for wrapping round each separate straw, so as to form the 'cords' which give a smooth, regular appearance. The best advice we can give you is to examine the old, worn-out cords you have removed; this will teach you the secret of making them. You have, in fact, to spin your own cords. The Great Reedmace, *Typha latifolia*, a semi-aquatic plant growing in marshes and on the edges of rivers, streams and ponds is extremely useful. Its seed-heads, dark chestnut in colour, look very well in a bouquet of dried plants. Its long, narrow leaves are thin and supple and, when twisted, make excellent cords for an out-and-out rustic style of seating. The leaves should be tied in bundles and left in a dry, well-ventilated place for some time, to prepare them for use.

The essential materials, then, for one chair seat: 250 grammes of straw cut at the knots, and 500 grammes of long straw.

Tools required are minimal and will have to be home-made; they cannot be bought.

Using holly or boxwood, both of which are hard and smooth, make an awl about 20 cm long and a spatula some 25–30 cm long. Add a good pair of scissors or a sharp knife, and your equipment is complete.

Preparing the straw and the chair

The day before you intend to start, slightly dampen both lots of straw: the long, uncut straw, and that which is cut at the knots. The object is to make it more pliable and easier to work with.

Take the nails out of the edging pieces (the thin wooden strips round the seat); remove the edging pieces and the old straw; clean up the rails. You are now ready to begin.

Patience is required

You won't get the knack straight away. But after a certain amount of experience you will find that re-seating a chair takes you only a few hours – about three. At first you may have to allow much longer; there is no blinking the fact that the work is of the slow, laborious kind and that you will often have to undo what you have done in order to make it as perfect as desired.

Don't let this fuss you; persevere patiently; you will learn to conquer all the little snags. You will have to sit on something fairly low in order to be at the right height in relation to the rails of the chair, with your straw on the ground beside you.

The first step is to take about twenty long straws and encase them (see later) in a piece of short rye straw (the straw divided into pieces at the knots). To do this, slit the short piece of rye along its length with your thumb-nail. What you have to construct is a kind of string or cord with a spiral wrapping: the short straw, converted into a flat band, is to enclose the long straws so that only the wrapping is visible. We shall refer to the result as 'the cord'.

When you get near the end of the long straw, splice another one to it; carry on in the same way, producing what looks like an

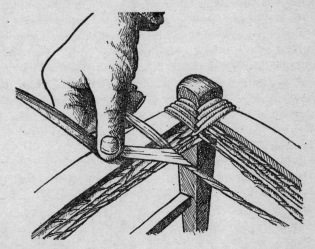

endless ribbon which, in unrolling, has remained twisted round an endless axis. The difficulty is that the cord has to be of uniform thickness throughout its length.

To re-cap: the split rye straw must surround the long straws, without gaps, the purpose of the long stems being simply to constitute the core or filter which is the foundation of the cord. When you have used up one piece of split straw, tuck the end in between the long stems and do the same with the next piece of split straw before you start winding it round the core.

Now put the cord on the chair. It is imperative to adhere faithfully to the path it is to describe in relation to the rails of the chair. Wind the cord twice round the right back leg of the chair (which is facing you on your left); stretch it tight towards the left back leg. Pass it once only round the frame and bring it towards the left front leg, then towards the right front leg, and lastly return it to the right back leg. You have now completed the first circuit.

Be careful: the back of the seat is narrower than the front, and you have to bring your work to a square shape. Therefore the next seven or nine circuits must be made as follows: one circuit on sides and front only; one circuit on all four sides, then one circuit on three sides; again one circuit on all four sides; one circuit on three sides; and so on, until you have achieved a perfect square. You then carry on, making circuits round all four sides and taking care to keep the cord tight between each leg and the next.

Generally, the whole seat will be covered by from forty to fifty circuits. If the work is done well it will finish with the cord at the mid-point of the front or back. The cord is then slipped under the other cords with the help of the bodkin and its end is cut off under the seat. This is the correct way of 'stopping' the end and completing this part of the work.

Finishing off

The next step is to turn the chair upside down and use odd pieces of the long straw for stuffing into the interstices between the cords.

Use your spatula for this. Properly inserted, this stuffing makes all tight and firm.

Turn the chair the right way up again and work on it with the flat end of your bodkin. This is probably the trickiest part of the whole operation, on which success depends.

Slip the bodkin between each cord and its neighbour in such a way as to press the cords evenly together. Your movements should be firm, regular and forceful.

Your work will be first-class provided all the cords are of equal thickness, packed close together, uniform in appearance and under strong tension.

The final step is to snip off any ends of long straw protruding under the seat.

You can also if you like, give your work one or two coats of a light golden-brown varnish, heavily diluted.

Re-upholster that old armchair

Re-upholstery is not very difficult. What you need is: a good pair of tailor's scissors, a packing-bar (failing which, a good screwdriver will do), a tack hammer (the really sophisticated craftsman uses a magnetic hammer; the heads of the tacks stick to it and he doesn't give himself blisters by constantly handling them), a curved needle for difficult places, and a wooden mallet for hitting the packing-bar.

Don't rip off the old cover haphazardly. Some of the nails would be left in, causing awkward bumps. Proceed in an orderly way. The vital thing is to strip the chair cleanly. Take the old cover off in one piece, so that you can use it as a pattern.

With the packing-bar (or the screwdriver) take out brass-headed nails, using a turn of the wrist. If tacks were used, the same tool will get them out but should be applied like a cold chisel and tapped sharply with the mallet. Pincers won't be necessary, except perhaps to extract a tack whose rusty head has come off when assaulted with the packing-bar.

Having removed the cover and nails (or tacks), inspect the calico, webbing and stuffing. Obviously, to renew the stuffing and the webbing, perhaps the springs as well, would demand a professional standard of skill. Just bring the general condition up to scratch by carefully refixing pieces of calico which confine the animal and vegetable fibres constituting the stuffing. If need be, recondition the stuffing by breaking it up wherever it has been felted together by long use, and add a handful of new stuffing here and there if you think it necessary – especially over the webbing and in the middle – fixing it with the curved needle to the inside of the calico.

If your armchair is antique, its stuffing will be in the old style, that is to say without springs but embodying a down cushion on top. The webbing will be fixed on the *upper* side of the rails, not

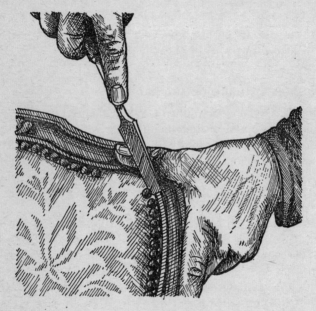

the bottom, as in sprung chairs. Hence you will find the webbing in direct contact with the hair stuffing. Tighten the straps one by one, if they need it. Sprung chairs are simple: the webbing is easy to find (on the underneath, covered with a single thickness of calico).

After these preliminaries, the next stage is to cut out the new cover, using the old one as a pattern. A good tip is to iron it lightly first; with the passage of years it will have acquired a shape of its own and will be almost impossible to lay out flat on the new piece of stuff. It is as well to leave a margin of 1 or 2 cm all round.

The order of operations is: first, the back; then the sides and arms; finally the seat. Having cut out the new pieces with the old as a guide you will have no difficulties. To be on the safe side you can tack on the new cover provisionally, using a larger size of tack and not driving them right in. If all is well, put in the full complement of smaller tacks and pull out the few big ones which you used for the trial fitting.

The arms

These, like curved parts in general, are a little tricky. The amateur usually goes first for the convex side, because it is outside and immediately visible. This is wrong. *Start with the inner, concave side.* You will have no difficulty in accommodating the superfluous stuff and avoiding the necessity for making darts on the convex side. Simply make a series of tiny gathers, very close together; these are easily hidden by brass-headed nails, or braid.

Put in these nails as soon as you have finished covering the chair. If your aim is uncertain and you frequently hit the wood, protect it with a stout piece of cardboard, held in the other hand. Many armchairs, however, are not completed with nails but with braid, which gives an excellent finish, covering any imperfections at the edges and also the heads of the tacks. Don't cut the braid where it turns a corner; fold it over, making a tuck. Use one of the latex adhesives and spread it in lengths of 15–20 cm at a time (it dries very quickly); put it only on the braid, which will stick instantaneously. Adhesive braid of excellent quality has recently started making its appearance, but the colour range is still rather too restricted to be much use for restoring antiques.

Sundry tips

Your tools must be very clean. A slightly rusty hammer, or an awl which has been used for opening a tin of paint or has lain on a greasy bench, would mark the material.

With satins and other fabrics which crease easily, a flannel lining is necessary. It need not be nailed but can be tacked to the calico with big stitches and, if you like, stuck at the edges with latex.

The edges of the material are likely to fray. Stick the frayed threads together with adhesive; they can then be trimmed with a razor-blade or a Stanley knife without danger of their fraying again.

Tapestry is often difficult to work, to stretch, or to lay over a curved surface. Make it supple by dampening the back. Stretch it in all directions to loosen the fibres. Leave it to dry on a board, first fixing it with pins to prevent it from shrinking.

To be surer of your positioning when putting on the material, use a stapler (stapling gun). Staples don't damage the wood and are easy to take out, and it is as if you had been given an extra hand with which to pull the stuff tight; otherwise, with a hammer and a nail to cope with, you must either neglect this essential aspect of the job or have someone to help you.

A recent innovation is a 'nail guide', made of plastic, which makes it easy to put in brass-headed nails at exactly equal distances.

6 Copper and brass

Copper

The leading interior decorators have an unjustifiable prejudice against copper. True, one does all too often encounter those pseudo-countrified displays which, headed by the inevitable copper kettle and running through a line of saucepans of different sizes, crown a mantelpiece or some other favourite position; the whole effect, at once vulgar and hackneyed, essaying to mimic Ye Olde Worlde Inn.

This very widespread material has been used for making innumerable household articles such as kettles, saucepans and warming pans. It is unusual to encounter it in objects with a decorative as well as a functional role, such as candlesticks, candelabra, ewers and so on, possibly because brass looks something like gold and was preferred for decorative items. This is one of the few cases in which our ancestors' logic was at fault; it was well known that copper was poisonous, especially when in contact with organic substances such as fat and oil. Its toxicity, though exaggerated by people, made it essential for the inside of kitchen utensils to be tinned.

Brass is an alloy of copper and zinc. The Gauls are thought to have been familiar with it after the Roman conquest, and to have distinguished it clearly from bronze. It seems that the great civilizations of the Mediterranean and the Middle and Far East were unacquainted with it, producing it only by accident when making bronze.

What is certain is that, in northern Europe, the cradle of the brass industry was Dinant in Belgium and the region of Namur. The word *dinanderie* was the generic term for everything made of brass from the early Middle Ages to the Renaissance. This localization is chiefly to be explained by the abundance of zinc ore (calamine) in the valley of the Meuse, though it was not until the sixteenth century that the metal itself was isolated and named by Paracelsus.

Until then, the ore was regarded merely as an additive which lightened the colour of copper. And it was only in the nineteenth century that a chemist in Liège, the Abbé Daniel Dony, invented a rational method of extracting zinc from calamine (zinc carbonate), Napoleon I having granted him the concession of the mine at Moresnet (near Liège and Verviers).

Thus for centuries copper and zinc were combined in an alloy empirically, the nature of one of the ingredients remaining substantially unknown. Contemporary documents show that brass was manufactured at Dinant in the eleventh century. But that town did not long retain the sole privilege: Lyon, Beaucaire and Paris manufactured *dinanderies*. So did certain centres in Auvergne. The Belgians' technique reached Italy and Milan had a very active community of *dinandiers*; likewise some of the German states. England has also had a long tradition of fine brass and copper work, and these crafts had received a stimulus from the immigration into the country of the gipsies, early in the sixteenth century. It is estimated that there are still some 15,000 gipsies in the United Kingdom. It is curious to note the present-day survival of the art of the coppersmith and brassworker among certain gipsy tribes of Spanish origin, now scattered in considerable numbers all over Europe. In France, members of that people are to be found at Saint-Ouen, the home of the *Marché aux Puces*, the celebrated 'Flea Market' of Paris. A specially interesting point is that in Spain coppersmithing is one of the *artes flamencos*, Flemish arts. Does this indicate a connection between the dinanderies of Flanders and the gipsies of Iberia?

Copper ancient and modern

Old and modern copper are easy to tell apart. In the past, all work in copper was achieved by patiently hammering an ingot on a former. As the metal was gradually drawn out by the hammer it was heated from time to time, to restore its malleability by annealing. The article thus produced was not uniform in thickness.

However, not all utensils could be shaped in one piece; pots and pans could, but urns, narrow-necked ewers and so on could not, and the joins were always visible. The brazing metal employed for copper having usually been brass, the line of the join is easy to detect and, incidentally, is seen more often than not to be crenellated, thus extending the area of contact.

Modern copper articles are made from sheet copper produced by a rolling mill to a uniform thickness. The old coppersmiths always made the bottom of the utensil thicker than the rest, both as a precaution against wear and in order to hold the heat, especially in the case of cooking vessels. These features are absent in modern copperware – its manufacturers know perfectly well that it is purely decorative in function.

But the traditional coppersmiths, such as the gipsies, while themselves using industrially manufactured copper stock, still braze their work in the old way.

Distrust any article in which the join consists of a seam (which is made by turning the metal back on itself and hammering the two parts together to make all tight and secure). The technique itself is not new, but it represents an easy way out which you are more likely to find in a modern piece than an old one. Finally, the following points to watch are as important as those we have already given:

Copper vessels soldered with tin should usually be rejected, unless the objects are not intended for use on the fire; examples are watering cans and urns, only the tap and the knob on the lids of which should be soldered, not the body of the urn (except in the case of repairs). The coppersmiths of bygone days made and brazed and soldered these decorative objects with special care. You should also beware of any ostentatiously beautiful repoussé work. The old craftsmen did sometimes embellish their pieces with repoussé but usually engraved these motifs as well, and

foliage and stylized flowers are encountered more often than elaborate coats of arms.

Reject without argument anything on which the hammer marks are absolutely regular; this is a sign of machine production for the cheap trade. Even articles whose hammering, though obviously done by hand, is too prominent, should be shunned; someone has been trying too hard! Craftsmen in the old days accepted hammering as their technique because it was necessary, but always did their best not to let it show.

If you find an article with one or more tubular handles, check for the presence of a longitudinal join in each of them. If there is none the article is modern: the maker has availed himself of a piece of copper pipe, as used in plumbing.

For a variety of reasons, economic and technical – notably the irregular thickness which distinguishes antique copper – modern copperware is perceptibly lighter than the genuine article.

The gipsies as tinkers

The most convincing hypothesis concerning the origin of the gipsies, those perpetual wanderers, is that they came from India, their migration westwards having begun about when prehistory ended. They are traditionally supposed to have brought the use of bronze to the Mediterranean countries. As late as 1332, the Englishman Simon Worcester made the first historical mention of these wandering tribes, at which date they were in Cyprus and appear to have been established there much earlier. Not until 1427 is their presence recorded in Paris and, more especially, at nearby Saint-Denis (where they have been ever since) and Pontoise. Harried wherever they went, it was only in northern Europe, or to be precise in Poland, that they were given rights (and also obligations). They were allowed to follow three trades, of which they held a virtual monopoly; those of the farrier, the locksmith and the tinker. This tolerance spread to the princely courts of Germany, where their skill was esteemed, and for some unexplained reason the same situation arose in Turkey, where to this day they are in almost exclusive control of the trades, and the premises of the brass-founder, the tinker and the farrier.

Braziers (brass-workers)

By a kind of unspoken convention, the work of the coppersmith and tinker is always thought of separately from that of the brazier. While there is no conclusive justification for the distinction, it serves to underline the higher value, and in some cases the greater antiquity, of certain work in brass.

Broadly, the division is as follows. The coppersmith or tinker was responsible for kitchen utensils: pots, kettles, preserving pans, stewpans, saucepans, cake moulds, dishes, ladles and the like, urns (sometimes ornate) and warming pans. The brass-worker was concerned with lighting: candlesticks, candelabra and lanterns; and with such work as bordered on the province of the goldsmith: ewers, including the small kind for hand washing (aquamaniles), censers and so on.

The objection to this rigid classification is that, in practice, coppersmithing covered all work done by forming and drawing out a sheet of metal, whether copper or brass.

The real technical difference between the coppersmith and the brazier was that between hammering and casting. It is clear at a glance that many antique lighting devices, and even some receptacles, were made in moulds. This applies to most candlesticks

Kettle from Beaucaire

prior to the eighteenth century; the so-called 'Dutch' candelabra; *conquemars* (a kind of kettle); the 'Beaucaire' kettles, characterized by their having two spouts and by the leonine or grotesque heads with which the hinges of the handle are ornamented (despite the name, Beaucaire was not the only place where they were made); and some other things. The techniques were often combined: the pillar or stem of a candlestick would be cast, the base hammered, and the whole finished and polished on the lathe. Details on candelabra were heightened with the chisel. Hollow forms were frequently used to avoid unnecessary weight; the two halves were beaten to shape and joined like the halves of a shell. Some people dogmatically assert that the brass-workers always stuck to a single, specific technique, but this is not tenable. We have seen examples of cast brass, others which were hammered to shape on a former, and yet others produced by stamping, a method akin to forged ironwork. Some amateurs nevertheless scrutinize brass candlesticks for signs of brazing or soldering as a visible sign of antiquity. These signs are not always present and nothing is proved by their absence.

Certain subsidiary indications, of a purely technical character, will tell you more.

Screw threads

Antique candlesticks are usually in two parts, the column (stem) and the base. In some cases the spindle on which the socket (candleholder) and sconce (disc for catching grease) are

mounted is screwed directly into the base. All the various parts are held together by screw threads, which, in antique work, have a characteristic form. The 'lands' of the thread are a bit rudimentary, have no sharp edges and are rather stout; the grooves between them are broad and flat bottomed. Take a good look at the threads on any antique piece of established authenticity, and you will always be able to recognize them thereafter. They also occur on 'Dutch' candelabra, to fix the sconces to the branches.

Structure of candelabra

The 'Dutch' candelabra, a triumph of Flemish art, have had an exemplary career. Their design remained virtually unaltered and was uneclipsed for at least four centuries, and it is sometimes extremely difficult to date them with any certainty. However, here is an attempt at classification.

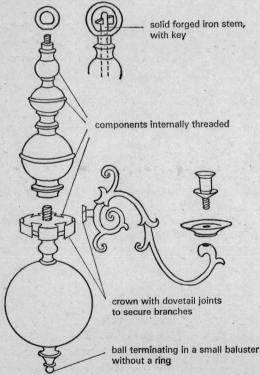

solid forged iron stem, with key

components internally threaded

crown with dovetail joints to secure branches

ball terminating in a small baluster without a ring

Prior to the eighteenth century:

the components are joined together either by large threaded portions cut in the main body of the metal, or are pierced by a solid forged iron stem and held in place by a key or cotter which is a force-fit in a key-way in the stem and secures the upper ring;

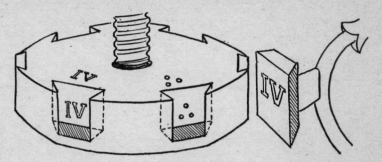

the branches are removable, being simply dovetailed into sockets in the crown which supports them. Sometimes their position is marked with a Roman figure engraved with the burin, or drawn with punchmarks, the same figure being repeated either on the top surface of the crown or in the female portion of the dovetail;

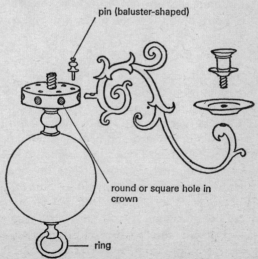

pin (baluster-shaped)

round or square hole in crown

ring

usually the bail at the bottom ends in a baluster-shaped motif, *with no ring.*

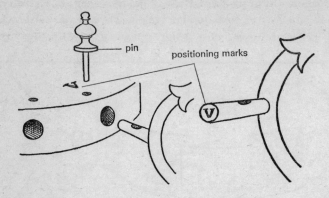

In the eighteenth century and early nineteenth century:
the components are joined together as before, by internal threads in the main body and a solid forged stem;

the arms, still removable, fit into the crown by means of round holes or square mortises and are fastened to it by little keys like balusters or ninepins. Positioning marks are as before, except that Arabic numerals are now sometimes used and that the marks are stamped on the tenon of the arm and on the underside of the crown;

a ring is usually fitted under the ball.

In the nineteenth century, candlelight became obsolete; gas lighting had been invented and the classical 'Dutch' candelabrum design was adapted to accommodate it. Hollow branches, to supply gas to the burners, were an unavoidable innovation; their shapes were gradually softened and became adulterated, departing further and further from the original. Holders with clips (claws) were added, to accommodate the opaline globes. The branches were round in section and in some cases had taps. No common type can be defined. Different combinations, unrelated to those preceding them, developed simultaneously. Further development arose with the coming of electricity. Branches became solid again, and sconces, as if for candles, returned. These candelabra were adapted often satisfactorily for electricity by means of wires with transparent insulation, *glued* to the branches and unobtrusively hugging their curves. The sconces were fitted with imitation candles and 'flame' bulbs. The branches were of course no longer dovetailed or keyed to the crown but usually held by screws from the inside of the crown, and the whole assembly was mounted on a tubular rod.

Copies of genuine candelabra exist, and are becoming more common in the stock of dishonest antique dealers. Common sense

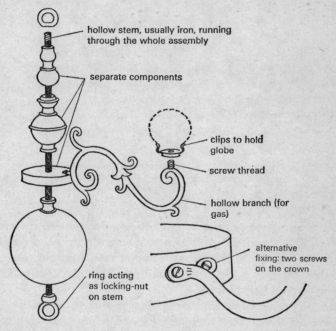

hollow stem, usually iron, running through the whole assembly

separate components

clips to hold globe

screw thread

hollow branch (for gas)

alternative fixing: two screws on the crown

ring acting as locking-nut on stem

should soon put you right about them. Remember that a candelabrum which is several hundreds of years old has seen a good deal of service, will have been polished innumerable times and is bound to show signs of its past.

Further remarks

A dolphin with another dolphin's tail in its mouth, or several such pairs, are a motif often found on the branches of 'Dutch' candelabra (other motifs, notably foliage, are also found, but dolphins are the most common).

Mosque lamp. The ring supports a coloured glass in which a wick is arranged to float on oil.

An interesting comparison is that between dolphins on the arms of candelabra and the well-known 'devouring monsters' which figure so largely in Viking culture. It is natural to wonder whether there is a decorative tradition common to the Low Countries and Scandinavia.

'Dutch' candelabra frequently display one or more specific symbols. The one most frequently found is an eagle with outspread wings, either on each of the branches or, which is more usual, at the top, just below the ring. These symbols are simply the emblem of the Hanseatic towns, of which Dinant was one. In various other centres where candelabra were made, the motif was repeated for purely decorative reasons.

Most antique 'Dutch' candelabra found in England were imported, but a considerable industry has existed here since the late seventeenth century, turning out candelabra of this type with all

dolphin motif

foliage motif (baroque; late)

the decorative motifs, or variations of them, shown in the illustrations. They have always been considered desirable as being handsome and long lasting. The workmanship of the early ones enables them to stand up to any but the most violent of rough usage.

The Virgin and Child, especially in the Middle Ages, are another motif occurring in 'Dutch' candelabra, at the top.

You may come across a candelabrum of 'Dutch' type whose arms are simply let into mortises in the crown, and in which the brass has been left rough from the file instead of being polished. Usually there is no ball and sometimes no sconces. Each arm ends with a ring which holds a coloured glass, in which a wick is arranged to float on oil. This type is an Oriental variant known as a 'mosque lamp'.

If you look at Flemish painting from Van Eyck to Vermeer, you will see that the many interior scenes depicted often include copper or brass objects, showing great detail.

Cleaning and preserving copper

Grossly oxidized copper

Suppose you find an antique copper vessel. Whatever it happens to be – a kettle, an ancient alembic, a watering can, a hand pump, a warming pan, a jug – it is thick enough with verdigris and dirt to discourage the stoutest heart.

There are various mixtures, all much alike, for resuscitating ancient copper; our own recipe is the following:

Dissolve some potassium oxalate crystals in water in the proportion of one-third crystals to 2 litres of water. If you can't get potassium oxalate, substitute hydrochloric acid but make sure the water is very hot. If possible, immerse the copper article. Otherwise, wet some cloths in the mixture and wrap them round it. The effect usually occurs quickly; as soon as the bare metal appears, rinse, then polish with any good commercial metal polish.

Strong bleach in boiling water is also very effective, providing the object to be stripped can be immersed in it.

Severe oxidation will certainly not be completely removed by any of these recipes. You must tackle it with pumice powder or a metal scouring pad (used cautiously), before repeating the above treatment.

Here is a folk recipe which has been found satisfactory by generations of people. Put a handful of sea salt in a saucer and pour over it a little less than enough boiling vinegar to dissolve all of it. Rub the copper with this mixture but do not let the mixture run down. You will see the oxidized patches progressively brightening and will have perfect control over the stripping.

Washing soda crystals or an ordinary detergent powder (two

handfuls to a litre of water) produce a deep, thorough cleansing action. Take a receptacle large enough to allow complete immersion of the article to be treated; place the article in it and fill up with the liquid; then bring to the boil, watching the effect from time to time. Follow this by thorough rinsing, then polish.

How to make copper really bright

If you are determined to make up your own polishing mixture, here are two recipes which can be recommended with confidence. Either should be used only on badly tarnished copper, not on anything which has been regularly polished.

Recipe 1: make a paste with tripoli and water to which about 20 per cent of oxalic acid has been added. Rub your copper items vigorously with this; finish off with a clean rag.

Recipe 2: mix 30 grammes oxalic acid with 100 grammes water. Add 40 grammes charcoal, 30 grammes alcohol (90 per cent) and 20 grammes turpentine. This results in a blackish paste which is excellent for restoring badly tarnished copper to its proper colour.

The secret of lasting brilliance

This consists of perfect polishing, whose stages are described below, *plus* a technical trick.

'Cleaning the copper' used to be an annual event carried out in late spring, in accordance with a well established ritual which has our entire approval.

The first stage consisted of cleaning all the articles with liquid metal polish and giving them a good rub. Next they were polished with dry tripoli. Finally, the polishing was finished with Spanish whiting to produce a dazzling brilliance.

But this was not all. To coax a warm glow from brass, and to 'fix' the brilliance of copper, all the articles were exposed to the sun for a few hours. The effect was magnificent.

The best manufactured polishes in the world can never replace this series of operations. Public Enemy No 1 for copper and brass is carbonic acid, and hence the carbon dioxide mixed with the humidity of the atmosphere. A rough measure of the increase in atmospheric pollution is provided by the frequency with which

copper articles now need polishing, especially in urban surroundings; a few decades ago, once a year was quite enough.

Today, you can keep your copper and brass items permanently
bright by giving them a coat of transparent colourless varnish,
obtainable either in small tins or bottles or in atomizer dispensers;
the latter are by far the best for applying an invisible uniform
film.

Note: All the methods for polishing and burnishing pewter are
also applicable to brass and copper, and the reader is referred to
the chapter in question.

7 Crystal

Crystal

Legend has it that, in some remotely ancient period, a party of merchants who had landed on the coast of Phoenicia used blocks of saltpetre to prop up their cooking pot, and that the saltpetre became fused with sand from the shore to create a hitherto unknown substance: glass.

In reality, glass was known in the countries of the East as early as 3000 B.C. The custom of burying glass objects in tombs appears to have been common both to Southern Egypt and to Assyria. Aristotle mentions that in Greece there were 'glass mirrors lined with polished metal'. Our own 'silvered' mirrors could hardly be better described.

The Latins, who were better at copying than inventing, began by importing glass from Egypt; later, in Nero's reign, it was manufactured in Rome. A large number of glass factories sprang up in 'the capital of the world'; it is even thought that, by 210 A.D. there was a glassmakers' quarter in the city. Glass was turned on the lathe; it was also carved, like silver. It was used for covering interior walls in houses, probably in the form of mosaics. Everyday Roman glassware consisted of drinking cups, perfume bottles, perfume jars and so on. In the catacombs, objects known as 'Christian glassware' have been found which are engraved with religious scenes and symbols.

In the tenth century of our era the most beautiful glass was imported from the East by the Venetians; early in the thirteenth century Venice herself became the largest Western centre of glassmaking.

In England, until the middle of the sixteenth century, all glass of any quality was imported from Italy, Holland and France. In about 1555, Jean Carré of Loraine, who had worked in both

Holland and France, was encouraged to come to England and set up a manufactory in the Weald. Later he moved to London and established the glasshouse in Crutched Friars. On his death, local jealousy drove his family out of London, and they settled in Newcastle and Stourbridge where glass has been made without interruption ever since.

In 1570, the Venetian, Giacomo Verzelini came to London and was granted a monopoly to manufacture 'Venice glass' on condition that he would teach English glassblowers his mysteries. Once the factory was established, all further imports from abroad were forbidden.

In 1674, George Ravenscroft began manufacturing a new type of glass which contained lead and was altogether stronger and more serviceable. Gradually it began to supplant the more brittle earlier wares. In the eighteenth century, as a result of a heavy tax imposed on glass, many manufacturers moved to Ireland, where Irish glasshouses flourished, and still do to this day. But it was during the nineteenth century in France that the industry developed on a large scale and reached a huge public as a result of significant technical improvements such as the Siemens furnace; another result was the rediscovery of lost secrets, for example those of iridescent glass and spun glass.

This was the period which saw the establishment of the chief French makers of crystal and cut glass (at Saint-Louis and Baccarat, 1819; and the firm of Daum at Nancy, 1875). Comparable glass was also being produced at this time in England, at the Stourbridge, Sowerby and Whitefriars factories.

It has often been asserted that these establishments are concentrated in eastern France not because of the deposits of potash, a necessary ingredient in the composition of crystal, but because the vast woodlands of the Vosges supplied fuel for the furnaces. Anecdotal sources confirm that, in those days, every glass factory had more woodcutters that glassworkers on its payroll. An odd fact, worth underlining, is that the siting of a glass factory has never been conditioned by that of the raw material. Venice, for instance, imports sand from which to make its famous crystal; and this sand comes from Fontainebleau!

The working temperature for crystal is its melting point,

between 1200 °C and 1400 °C. The glassblower picks up the right amount of molten crystal with his blowpipe and transfers it to a cast-iron mould. The mould is hermetically closed; he applies his mouth to the other end of his blowpipe and blows, to make the crystal conform itself snugly to the interior. When it has cooled, he will have obtained the cup of (let us say) a wineglass. He then takes more molten crystal and draws it out to the required length to form the stem; after which he takes another lot of crystal and flattens it to make the foot. From these three he puts together the embryonic wineglass.

This is passed on to the grinder for trimming. Every grinding operation is specifically conceived for its purpose. The speed of rotation will depend on the fineness or coarseness of the wheel selected, which in turn depends on the effect required. A carborundum wheel will be needed for the first trim. For cutting, a wheel of Alsatian grit-stone (*grès d'Alsace*) will be sufficient. Corundum, a porcelain agglomerate, is another material used for grinding-wheels.

Next the piece will be polished on a wheel made of wood, and another of natural or compressed cork; after which it will be engraved with little cutters tipped with grit-stone, sand or emery, very like a dentist's drill. The finished glass, in its inimitable transparency, is now ready to take its place on your table or in your collection.

This technique produces perfectly uniform shapes. But there is nothing to stop you preferring the less stereotyped forms produced by master glassblowers who reject moulds and multiple polishings in favour of greater freedom. The piece is shaped by blowing and by an ingenious and variable combination of movements in the air and of rotating it on a smooth surface (the 'marver', a metal or marble plate). Of course the result is imperfect, in a sense. There will be bubbles in the glass, the contours will be a little irregular, and there is no chance whatsoever of your being given a complete service consisting of identical pieces. But does that matter? If you really love crystal or glass, you will be happy for the material to impose its own laws on the technique, not conversely (and rigidly). What a pleasure it is to lay a table on which every *couvert* preserves, amid the general

harmony, its own individuality and life instead of servilely dupli-
cating its neighbours!

Identifying glass and crystal

The criteria which make it possible to tell crystal from ordinary
glass are quite unreliable unless backed up by considerable training. Wetting the rim of a glass and rubbing it with a finger to
make it vibrate and sound a musical note, is merely a parlour
trick. People say that genuine crystal produces a pure note, but
in fact this frequently depends on the shape of the object. Common glass is sometimes delightfully sonorous.

The main thing to realize is that crystal is much stronger than
glass (it contains lead, whereas glass contains barytes) but, as a
result of its composition, less elastic, more brittle.

Crystal and glass, in fact, are like dogs and cats: there are
various breeds, any individual specimen can be described in terms
of its origin, appearance and ancestry, and the price varies too.
Luckily, however, both have their own official studbook, as it
were: legal standards have been set up by which to classify them.
In France, the *norme* NF B-30004 differentiates them precisely in
terms of their refractive indices. (The refractive index expresses
the angle through which light rays are 'bent' by passing through
glass. The higher the index, the greater the degree to which light
is trapped by reflection and caused to 'play' within the refracting
medium.)

Let us explore the characteristics of crystal and glass.

Lead crystal is required by law to contain 24 per cent of lead.
Its metallic sonority (caused by its high lead oxide content), and
its brilliance, clarity and density make it the noblest material in
the whole range.

Crystal contains less than 24 per cent lead but is none the less a
noble material. Its refractive index is high and its purity, brilliance and sonority enable models of great beauty to be obtained
from it. Crystal vessels, deeply and richly cut, contribute to the
most refined of tables a charm and elegance acknowledged by all.

Crystalline has a lower refractive index but is a sonorous,
brilliant and very pleasing material. Finely cut and elegantly
shaped services, with decorative elements, are made from it.

Glass, with the lowest refractive index, is also the cheapest of these materials. Clear or coloured services can be produced in it, whose simple or elegant design gives pleasure in daily use.

To end our list, what is often called *demi-crystal* is a kind of glass intended to imitate crystal; its name is incorrect and illegal.

Crystal can only be produced by craftsmen and, in our mechanical age, is bound to be expensive. It is worth reflecting, as you sip your Saint-Emilion or Riesling, that the glass containing it may well have undergone a hundred and twenty different operations – details of which we forbear to give, yet could not leave wholly unmentioned.

Iridescent glass from excavations

The Mediterranean basin – Egypt, Mesopotamia, Palestine, Greece and Rome – has yielded up a number of objects which fascinate collectors and are in some instances of great antiquity; they include flasks, tear bottles, *alabastres* and the like. For the most part they are small, iridescent, elegantly shaped receptacles, not very transparent. In origin they are generally funerary, which explains their miraculous state of preservation, for they are fragile for more reasons than one.

As always, the faking industry has set itself to copy them: these fakes are manufactured in Venice, the Balearic Islands, Syria and probably wherever glassblowers are still to be found.

Luckily the fakes are fairly obvious. They are always heavier than the genuine thing, whose extreme lightness is always immediately impressive. Moreover they are blown in a single operation, whereas very ancient glass was fashioned by a different technique. A core of clay was coated with molten glass; when the glass had cooled the core was washed out of the vessel built up round it. Sometimes the core was held in shape by a jacket of fine gauze. Traces of this device appear in the result, especially as the glass was applied in successive layers. This causes the highly characteristic leafy tracery exhibited by this species of glassware. The inner surface of the vessel often displays concretions, usually calcareous, and these deposits are rather unskilfully reproduced by the fakers. Genuine examples, because of the long, slow process by which they were built up in successive layers, show variations in thickness and colouring; the fakes do not. The faker uses the same colouring matter throughout; usually a mixture of white-wash and ochre.

Later, almost certainly in the last two centuries of the pagan era, and probably in Greece, the technique of glassblowing was discovered. But the extreme lightness of the results, and the nature of the concretions, none the less provide a sound pointer to the age of any given piece.

Rock crystal

The glassblowers' crystal must not be confused with rock crystal. The latter is a natural chemical compound, a variety of quartz, substantial quantities of which occur in a few deposits in the Alps, Brazil and Madagascar. Rock crystal is appreciably harder than its near namesake; it can be worked only with special diamond-faced grinding-wheels. There is, indeed, an interesting degree of resemblance between diamonds and rock crystal: the sites where they are found are geologically similar, and the refractive index of both substances is high.

Rock crystal has been used from very early times for making precious objects like jewellery and amulets; it occurs in medieval reliquaries; later still, it was the material preferred for the costliest lighting assemblies – candelabra, chandeliers and ornamental candlesticks. Specialists with a great deal of experience can recognize rock crystal at a glance and do not mistake it for crystal. One can, in fact, on looking through rock crystal, detect a 'freckled' effect, presumably caused by its crystalline structure. Rock crystal is always worked by means of abrasion. You should therefore be able to find traces of this treatment not only on edges, motifs and facets but also on flat surfaces: though perfectly polished, there will be very slight departures from flatness here and there.

Repairing glass and crystal

There is no proper technique for this; only expedients. Of course you can stick broken pieces together again with two-part epoxy resin adhesives, but the join will always be visible (see directions for mending faïence and porcelain).

In some cases a break can be evened out by grinding, for example on the edge or foot of a glass, but this is a craftsman's job; you are unlikely to have the necessary equipment. Metal bands can be used to repair a really valuable piece. The foot of a stemmed glass which has been snapped clean off can be stuck on again and the repair concealed by a metal band. Fine work of this kind can also be applied to the neck or handle of a wine jug. Very few craftsmen are capable of such work.

However, there is one piece of advice which the amateur will find useful. When a piece is kept for display and never gets wet it can be simply and almost invisibly mended by using white of egg as an adhesive. This works well. Moreover, a one-stage (as against two-part) contact adhesive has recently been developed.

It takes only ten minutes to reach maximum hardness, a single drop will cover 6 cm, and because it has the same refractive index as glass it is invisible even when used for a large repair.

Looking after glass and crystal
Crystal, being so fragile, must be looked after with great care. Its greatest enemies are dust and clumsy washing up.

So the care required, though simple, is minute. There is always the danger of scratches, hence crystal should never be dusted when dry. It is always safe to remove dust by washing in luke-warm water, not by dipping in a bowl but by holding under a tap. A glass or vase should never be placed upside down on a hard surface, such as a draining board, without first covering the latter with a cloth or a sheet of foam rubber. This avoids chipping the rim. For drying, use a very soft cloth or a chamois leather.

8 Engravings

Engravings: how to restore them

Before proceeding to describe methods used in the trade to clean
prints and watercolours, we must warn the reader that the cleaning of valuable engravings should always be carried out by a
reliable expert. With practice and great care, you may come to be
an expert, but it will take time. Practise with some very cheap
prints that can be picked up for a few shillings on any junk
market. The methods given below have been used by dealers over
many years, but we repeat that to employ them successfully
requires considerable skill and practice.

You have acquired some engravings – you glanced inside a
portfolio in a junk shop or went treasure-hunting in a dusty attic,
or perhaps a relation left them to you in his will. Some of them are
infected with blotches of discoloration which blur the delicacy
of the drawing.

What can be done?

The commonest causes are age and damp. Occasionally, oil,
grease or rust are responsible. And there is sometimes damage
done by flies.

Provided you diagnose the origin of the blemishes it is easy to
rejuvenate the engraving by means of the handful of recipes
below.

Getting rid of oily stains

Take a sheet of blotting paper or other absorbent paper and dust
it evenly with Fuller's earth (if this is not available, use talc or
finely ground plaster). Then very carefully irrigate the stain with
turpentine, and lay the engraving face downward on the sheet
covered with Fuller's earth.

On the back of the engraving, opposite the spot, spread more

Fuller's earth. (Both in this and in the first operation, there is no need to put down a layer all over; it is enough to cover the area of the stain and a little more.) Then cover the whole with another sheet of blotting paper and place a suitable weight on top, such as a book or an ash-tray, and leave it for at least twenty-four hours.

If the results at the end of that time are poor, plug in the electric iron, setting it to 'silk' (if your iron has no thermostat, bring it to the heat suitable for the most delicate, vulnerable materials) and carefully iron the blotting paper (or other absorbent paper) until the stain vanishes. The same method can also be used on pencil drawings.

Getting rid of stains caused by mould

Fill a large bowl or a washbasin with a mixture composed of one part hydrogen peroxide (see page 6) 130 volumes (if unobtainable from a chemist, you will be able to get it from a cabinet makers' supplies merchant) and two parts distilled water. Take care not to use tap water, it has too much lime in it. Add a few drops of ammonia.

Lay the engraving on the liquid, into which it will gradually subside.

You should watch the print to see whether the treatment is being effective. The spots should begin to fade after five minutes. When the stains have vanished, lift out the print and lay it in a basin of distilled water, to wash out the peroxide. Lift it out after ten minutes and lay it on a glass to dry.

There is no answer to rust

Of all the stains that spoil an engraving, those caused by rust are certainly the least responsive to the known remedies. However, here are two which, if the stains are a little obliging, may well succeed.

Start by washing the engraving several times in lukewarm water, concentrating (cautiously!) on the stains. Then dust the stains with potassium oxalate. Finally, rinse thoroughly.

One can also try using the anti-rust preparations sold for laundry purposes.

Rust often defeats all attempts to remove it, so don't expect miracles. But you will probably have the satisfaction of making the stains much dimmer, even if they don't totally disappear.

Other stains

Stains resulting from damp make ugly inroads on engravings. Here are some methods used by skilled restorers.

Lay the engraving flat on the bottom of your bath, and cover it to a substantial depth with coarse sea salt from the kitchen. Cut up two or three lemons and squeeze the juice on to the salt. Don't be too economical, the salt must get adequately soaked in lemon juice. Leave for an hour or two, then rinse the engraving thoroughly.

Another method employs a mixture made up thus:

To every litre of water, add two tablespoonsful of chloride of lime and two tablespoonsful of soda crystals. Soak the engraving in the mixture, take it out and wait for ten minutes. Rinse thoroughly, as usual, but add a little vinegar to the water first.

Both these mixtures can also be used for treating an engraving which has yellowed slightly with age. But don't be over-optimistic. Neither of them will dramatically restore the paper to its original whiteness. The yellowing will diminish but may not vanish completely, however hard you try.

How to dry engravings during treatment

To dry an engraving, the best way is to use new blotting paper spread out on a really flat surface (such as the glass top of a desk) and simply lay the engraving on it. But remember to proceed very carefully, avoiding creases or dog's ears (bent corners), which, once made, may be permanent.

A large engraving can be dealt with by removing it from the water in which it has been rinsed and sticking it to one of the inside walls of the bath. It will automatically come unstuck when it has dried out.

Important: never expose a drawing or engraving to sunlight. It should always be allowed to dry slowly, in the shade.

Also rigorously avoid hanging it on a line; the clips or pegs would mark the paper.

Repairing a small tear

If, while treating an engraving, you tear the paper slightly, the damage is not catastrophic and can be made good.

Turn the engraving over and lay it flat, face downward, on a smooth surface. Then coat the edges of the tear with flour paste and apply a strip of paper 2 or 3 cm wide. Before putting the strip on, check carefully to make sure that the edges of the tear have met correctly. Leave the repair to dry for a few hours and then carefully tear off any spare tissue paper at either side of the join. If you are a perfectionist, very lightly smooth the repair with fine glasspaper; the damage will then be completely invisible.

In this kind of repair, never use ordinary sticky paper or plastic tape. In course of time it turns the paper yellow; it also shrinks and tears it.

Stains on a watercolour

As a general rule, stains or spots of any sort on a watercolour are practically impossible to remove. But there is one simple procedure which sometimes works, within limits. We pass it on with reservations.

In a tinting saucer (the kind of little porcelain dishes used by watercolour painters and others) or, failing this, in a large spoon, mix 5 drops of ammonia with hydrogen peroxide 20 volumes (see page 6).

Arm yourself with a fine brush with a good point; you can get this at an art shop. Dip it in the mixture and moisten the spot – and nothing else. Go very carefully. If you put on too much of the liquid, so that it overflows the frontiers of the spot, dry it quickly by dabbing very lightly with a bit of cottonwool.

You can apply the mixture three or four times in succession, but it is wise to let a few minutes elapse between applications.

Flies

The dirt deposited by flies is hard to remove, especially from paper. To make them less conspicuous and in many cases eliminate them, we would advise that you first scratch them with a photographic retouching pen (or, as explained in a later passage, a scarifier used by doctors for vaccinating). For good results, the paper must be perfectly dry. Don't overdo it on the most recalcitrant spots; just scratch the surface. The mixtures recommended here will then effectively complete the job.

9 Furniture

Pegs and what they tell us

Lovers of antiques who like to think they know it all, invariably pass an absent-minded finger over an imperceptibly protruding peg, or turn a chair upside down to inspect the state of the rails – and, of course, the pegs – as a guarantee of age and authenticity.

Fairly often, someone has got there before these enthusiasts and anticipated their scrutiny. This 'someone' is the antique dealer. In dealers' back-shops, pegging goes on with might and main: the public having discovered this infallible criterion of age, there is a natural anxiety not to disappoint them. Pegs are driven in all over the place; until, eventually, it dawns on the disconsolate customer that the 'infallible' criterion means precisely nothing. Nevertheless, the evolution of the peg as an aspect of the furniture maker's art is of particular interest. Pegging is a means of fixing two pieces of wood rigidly together, and in order to avoid giving this chapter an artificially over-specialized bias I shall try to show how the technique of construction has developed and changed with the passage of time. The fact that pegging became obsolete is in itself a useful pointer.

The middle ages

Really early furniture dating back to the Middle Ages (to which we can arbitrarily ascribe a term with the invention of printing from movable types in 1454) derives its lesser or greater importance for us from the intricacy of its Gothic carving, the nicety of its proportion, or the reverence due to its state of preservation. Except in the palaces of kings, cardinals and great nobles, it was simply an exercise in solid joinery, constructed to suit its purpose: a trencher table, a couple of benches and one solid high armchair for the master; great presses, fourposters.

Iron nails were not unknown (in countries obsessed with the Crucifixion, they could not be used) but in the construction of furniture such as it was in those days we find it holding a tenon in a mortise; but we also find it securing the crosspieces on the underside of the lid of a chest, or fixing a table top to the central upright. Carvings are often literally nailed on to furniture with a peg. When a panel consists of two or three sections, don't look for a chamfer or a tongue-and-groove; pegs will have been used, in some cases driven in obliquely.

During the seventeenth century the technique of pegging, though already very satisfactory, underwent a slight improve-

'Pigeons' in the lid of a chest

ment. In table tops and chest lids, and in every cabinet making operation requiring several boards to be joined together in a plane, countersunk fillets were introduced. Mortises are cut in the underside of the boards and a thin piece of wood, fitted flush, is pegged in to secure the flat assembly thus obtained. Sometimes, in a table top, you can see the pegs, usually in a circular formation, straddling the join.

Form follows function in the shaping of the peg, which is long and slim, tapers to a point and is thickest at the head. Usually it is of the same kind of wood as the piece as a whole. As you are never likely to take a piece of furniture to pieces and therefore to extract

the pegs, these details are somewhat academic. Still, pegs sometimes work their way out spontaneously; you will then be able to
verify our information and your own knowledge. It should be
noted that pegs were usually made from square dowel, which is
why the butt-end, or 'head' is square.

In the eighteenth century, cabinet making was further refined
and perfected. Dovetail joints were much used and mitred construction made its appearance (this is supposed to have been invented in the sixteenth century, but did not become current practice until much later). Marquetry became widespread under
Louis XIV; so did gilded furniture. Pegs were masked by veneer
or by gilding. It was the beginning of the end for the peg – a device
regarded as technically necessary but aesthetically displeasing.
However, it remained indispensable throughout the eighteenth
century, but those working for the aristocracy concealed their
pegs with carvings (especially on chairs, etc.), or with veneers,
which by this time were ruling the roost, or with lacquer, which
was a novelty.

Commodes and *semainiers* were even sent out unfinished to
China, where local craftsmen completed them. In 1748 two
brothers, Frenchmen by the name of Martin, invented a process
which was described at the time as producing varnishes '*façon de
Chine*'. Today, Martin's varnishes are famous (and are known in
English as well as French as *vernis Martin*). All these advances in
decoration tended towards greater refinement in both form and
technique.

English marquetry was, as will be seen, a late development. In
the Louis XIV period, its style was derived wholly from conti-
nental sources, mainly French. The elaborate French style was
itself derived from the Italian. Dutch influence came into England
with William of Orange, and Dutch marquetry, in many ways the
most exciting, was inspired by both Spain and Italy. For the
purely English manner of marquetry we have to get well into the
eighteenth century. A school of cabinet making developed whose
first creative figure was Chippendale, succeeded by artists like
Robert Adam, Thomas Sheraton and (pre-eminently) George
Hepplewhite, all of whom underwent the influence of the French
stylist. The goal towards which they strove was an almost ex-

cessive lightness of design, carried to such a pitch that the joints then commonly used would have been out of place in their arm-chairs with airily soaring backs, and their slender chairs with threadlike limbs. Sheraton refined the joints and avoided ordinary pegging as far as possible; he used grooved pins, and perfected the art of gluing by using the toothed plane, a complete novelty at the time. The blade of this type of plane cuts a number of triangular grooves and thereby doubles or trebles the area of contact and, in consequence, the holding power of the glue.

The way the plane works is perhaps made clearer if we add that it cuts regular furrows in both surfaces, and that the two surfaces then fit each other perfectly and are secured by gluing.

The nineteenth century was to sound the death knell of the peg; it was only accepted provided it was invisible. It can be found in

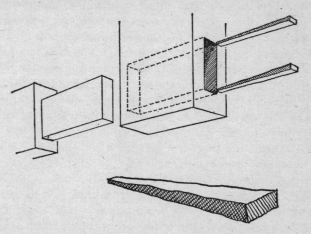

the woodwork of chairs upholstered all over, and frequently in the rails of chairs and armchairs, but only when the rails are covered up out of sight. The firmness of the backs and arms of chairs was obtained by using glue, the famous 'strong glue' (see the chapter on glues), a bone glue which was kept simmering, in a pot with a water-jacket, in every workshop.

In high-quality work an excellent device, wedging, in the special form of a fixed tenon, is used. A saw-cut is made in the end of the tenon and a small wooden wedge, slightly too long, is inserted in it; the tenon is then driven home in the mortise, the wedge being brought flush with the end of the tenon and causing it to expand, so that the joint is solid for keeps. It can never be taken apart, the only way to undo it would be to break and destroy it.

During the second half of the nineteenth century the cabinet maker's craft developed towards a technical perfection which robbed it of freshness and stifled the creative urge under a feather pillow of academicism. Imitation was the order of the day; alas, if only the craftsmen had contented themselves with straight-forward copying! Ossified decorative preferences, and technical difficulties, were promiscuously combined. Craftsmanship ruled triumphant; it had become an end in itself, instead of existing to serve art.

High-quality furniture was transmogrified into 'masterpieces', in the showmanship sense of that term: that is to say, the piece was regarded as an opportunity for the craftsman to show off all his knowledge and cunning at one go, without consideration for the general aesthetic effect. Artistic subtlety was ousted by craft virtuosity – and the next step was the industrialization of cabinet making, with all that followed from it.

The old tenon-and-mortise was almost completely replaced by dowel joints, it being easier to drill holes than make mortises. Screws were another short cut. Veneer was no longer an adorn-ment but a device for reducing cost. Wood, that noble material, was used as a façade to conceal shoddiness.

Reaction to this debasement of the true craft, and to the over elaborate and massive style of the age, came in both England and France. In England, William Morris (1834–1896) set an example of fine craftsmanship coupled with delicacy of design which was to be a powerful influence in the last years of the nineteenth and the first decade of the twentieth centuries, leading to the flowering of the 'Art Nouveau' movement. Morris had set up his factory (Morris, Marshall, Faulkner and Co) in 1858, with Rossetti, Burne Jones and Madox Brown as directors, in the full surge of the Pre-Raphaelite movement, and any piece of furniture from this factory is now keenly sought by collectors and highly priced. The movement spread to the provinces and was strongly taken up in Scotland, where Arthur J. Macmurdo was already, in the seventies and eighties, producing elegant furniture in the fullest 'Art Nouveau' style.

In France, the great Louis Marjorelle, though spurned by the manufacturers who persisted in producing tasteless and heavy reproductions of 'Pompadour' commodes and Henry II presses and sideboards, was to receive recognition in the early years of the twentieth century.

Today, the trademarks of Morris, Macmurdo and Majorelle can be set alongside those of the great masters of the past, such as Hepplewhite, Sheraton, Jacob, Cressent and Riesener.

For, despite appearances to the contrary, the pliant vegetable forms of the 'modern style' (as it was also called) are conceived in a spirit of profound discipline. The joints are the sound, traditional ones, with extra support to carry the projections and overhangs produced by the new freedom of design. Beautiful furniture is never badly made, though it does not necessarily follow that well-made furniture is beautiful. By concentrating on a single technical aspect, namely pegs and joints, and casting a few brief glances at the history of cabinet making from this point of view, we have been able to watch the development of an art. Every material has a logic of its own; this naturally imposes the techniques employed in the use of that material, in conjunction with the development of tools and equipment from one period to another.

After the first look at any piece of furniture comes the detailed examination. It requires no particularly expert knowledge to realize that:

the regular markings left by the modern band-saw make one a little suspicious of a supposed Louis XIII piece, even though it be efficiently pegged (sometimes newly so!);

the slightly wavy texture left by machine planing indicates either a modern fake or a clumsy piece of restoration;

the head of a peg which is lighter than the object as a whole implies that the pegs were added later and are therefore spurious;

pegs, even if much coated, as if by age, mean nothing if other features point to modern mass production (rear panels made of plywood; screws; carvings added to complete the effect, etc.);

excessively thin veneers are always an indication of cheap mass production;

nails (unless hand-forged) and screws are foreign to genuine antique furniture which has been well looked after;

Stripping cottage furniture

You fall in love with a rustic piece of furniture that you come across in the shop of a likeable dealer. You agree the price and buy the thing without examining it very closely. It's pretty dirty; the dealer says he found it in a chicken-house.

On closer inspection you find it is covered with that fearful dark brown paint of which the recipe seems to be known only to village painters; and the bottom rail and the feet have woodworm. To cap it all, the patina which you mistook for some kind of craftsman's finish is just a thick layer of dirt, polished by long use. So perhaps you feel disappointed. But why should you? A piece, whether it be furniture or anything else, remains dead or comes to life according to the amount of interest bestowed on it. How often have you not found that an object which looked like nothing at all in a dealer's window increases its value tenfold in your own home?

Get the dirt off first

The preliminary to all stripping is cleaning. Until you have got the superficial dirt off you can't tell much about what lies underneath it: the paint or varnish which you intend to remove.

Use a powder detergent and warm water, in the proportion of 50 grammes to a litre.

The things you need for any sizeable job of stripping are: a packet of washing powder, some caustic soda or caustic potash for stripping, a soft brush, a wire brush for clasps, locks, hinges, etc., a putty knife for grooves, carvings and so on.

Using a sponge, moisten the entire surface with the washing liquid (diluted as above). Leave it to work for a few seconds, then repeat, using a larger amount of liquid. Dirty carvings, if any, will defeat the sponge. This is where your soft brush comes in. It will be useful in various other ways before you have finished.

The washing liquid must be given a chance to 'bite'. Only pro-longed contact will enable it to do so. Soak a large rag, such as an old apron or flannel, in the liquid, clap it on and leave it long enough to take effect. Flour is often added to the liquid so as to make a flour paste; this sticks to the vertical parts of the piece and allows the cleaning to go on for as long as you want.

Strip furniture cautiously

Stripping with potash is very spectacular, but *dangerous* to the eyes and to sensitive skins. Certain precautions are necessary; don't neglect them. The first is simply: Be careful. Don't pour out too much of the stripping agent at one time. Wear spectacles and plastic gloves (not rubber – the potash will soon begin break-ing it down). If possible work out of doors, near a water supply. The potash should be diluted with warm water; in what propor-tion, will depend on the resistance of the paint (start by trying about two wineglassfuls of potash to a litre of water). Abundant froth is the sign that the potash is working. Don't rinse off the froth as fast as it appears, leave it to work. You will find that any carvings will have to be stripped in a horizontal position, so that the stripping agent can get into the crannies; so lay the object flat on its side or back. In places where the soft brush is not adequate, for example if the paint is too thick, use the putty knife.

If your chemist has no potash, substitute any of the products sold for unblocking a washhand basin. These products usually come in crystal form (the size of the crystals varies from one brand to another). Sprinkle the crystals over the surface of the piece (dry), ensuring good coverage everywhere; then pour very hot water over them. Use a watering can with a fine rose; too power-ful a stream would sweep the crystals away. The instantaneous result is a violent effervescence, and on rinsing down you will see that all traces of paint have vanished.

We repeat our safety warning. These products are powerful and effective but must not be handled carelessly. Splashes can be dangerous. Don't let children or pets come near you when you have a piece of furniture to strip.

After these successive applications, copious rinsing is essential. If you neglect this, the potash will 'bloom' in the form of minute crystals on the surface of the wood. The jet of a garden hose will enable you to get at the trickiest places.

Don't let the piece dry off yet, there is something very important still to be done. Potash, like a number of other substances, including ammonia, has the property of causing chemical reactions which make some kinds of wood turn darker in colour – it does so to oak, for example, and Spanish chestnut; cherry, on the other hand, turns red. *So the colour of the wood, denatured by the potash, must be lightened.* This is very necessary: if you were to wax-polish your piece of furniture at this stage the result would be a gloomy, greyish, matt tone, without gloss. There are several ways of restoring the colour to its natural lightness. Cabinet makers' suppliers sell peroxide (120 volumes) (see page 6), which is a powerful bleach (watch out for your fingers and clothes); an older method is to use an oxalic salt, which comes in the form of a white crystalline powder. Dust this on the piece while it is still damp. The salt acts almost immediately. To help it dissolve, so that the active principle can penetrate the wood, pour on hot water from a kettle.

A few minutes later, rinse through. The job is now done. The wood has gone back to its natural colour. The article can be left to dry (you will, of course, have taken the opportunity of cleaning the interior, such as drawers or shelves).

It is worth noting that one of the cabinet maker's recipes for lightening the colour of wood is to use hydrochloric acid, which makes oak produce a rather beautiful golden glow.

In praise of fine cabinet making

Fine furniture, with or without inlays or marquetry, has not always eluded the over-enthusiastic paintbrush or the efforts of the would-be improver. There are some almost unbelievable reasons for this and it is never a bad thing to pause for a second glance at some piece whose surprisingly elegant design is contradicted by a superficial appearance. I have seen a genuine Louis XV table of remarkable purity of style being used as a laundry bench by a

country washerwoman. To make it slope she had partially ampu-
tated two of the legs; a piece of wood had been nailed on to provide a ledge for her soap; and the whole had been carefully
painted white, 'to be nice and clean'!

This desire for so-called cleanliness is one of the worst enemies
of neglected, unloved furniture.

Undoubtedly, the refrigerators, washing machines and gas or
electric cookers which have invaded country kitchens in recent
years are out of keeping with traditional furniture, which therefore often gets dumped in an outhouse. Sometimes it gets ex-
changed for items with Formica tops by travelling furniture
dealers, shrewd operators well aware of being on to a good thing.
Alternatively, these antique pieces may simply be given a good
coat of enamel and garnished with 'contemporary' handles, etc.,
and be allowed to keep their place because they are useful. However, their disfigurement is not irrevocable.

A further cause of these bizarre expedients is the ravages of
time. Bits of inlay that have come unglued and got lost, lacquer
cracking or flaking, scars from burns: any or all of these may pro-
voke misguided repairs, usually in the form of camouflage. And
camouflage means paint, of course, often with a pseudo-genteel
finish in view, such as graining or imitation marble.

That dreadful black paint

This panorama of faulty taste and the crimes of ignorance would
of course be incomplete if we omitted the faults engendered by
fashion. In the early nineteenth century dark furniture was in
favour. Ebony being expensive, anything which looked like ebony
was accepted as a substitute. So everything was painted black;
and, at least, one is forced to admit that the paint was of such
good quality that the furniture of that period is as lustrous today
as when the paint was put on.

But the treatment was not confined to the output of contemporary cabinet makers; it was conscientiously applied to the
furniture of earlier periods.

In England, the overpainting of furniture with black paint
came somewhat later in the nineteenth century and was not due
to the dictates of bad taste, as it was in France. The death of the

Prince Consort, Albert, in 1861, plunged the country into a frenzy of mourning, in sympathy with the shattered Queen. In this crepe maker's hour, many of the royal widow's subjects were not content only to wear black, but sought to demonstrate the depths of their own grief and love by turning their parlours and drawing-rooms into mortuaries by the application of heavy black paint to anything that shone and to any furniture not strictly subfusc. Fortunately for the country's heritage, these macabre demonstrations were confined to the middle and especially the lower classes. The aristocracy knew better how to control their emotions and, however deep their feelings, did not feel called upon to desecrate their Chippendale commodes or Adam console tables.

Today, small pieces of good old furniture still turn up covered in paint, usually white, underlying which, when it comes to stripping, the mourning paint is discovered.

Today this black paint is the despair of many antique collectors especially when they encounter it on a piece of furniture which a dealer says was not like that 'from birth'.

Removing 'Louis Philippe' black

The equivalent to Louis Philippe black in England was the factory ebonized furniture of the period, for which, however, there was less demand than in France. The removal of this hard and highly polished surface presents the same problems as Louis Philippe black, and its removal often discloses really atrocious workmanship and quality of wood underneath.

This substance's tenacity, which we have often come up against, impressed us so much that we asked a technical laboratory to analyse it. We were told that it is not really a paint at all but a *lacquer varnish*, whose brilliant surface was obtained by the methods described in our chapter on French polishing.

Hence it sometimes responds to alcohol and can always be removed by a stripper containing acetone.

These strippers are easy enough to buy. They are put on with a brush but almost always need washing off afterwards. Can this always be done?

If you venture on the dangerous experiment of stripping a chair, armchair or some other kind of seat, at the same time protecting its upholstery, washing down is out of the question. Scraping is the only answer; and, as we shall see, it is the answer in most cases too, however slow and boring a business it may be.

If you use a cabinet maker's scraper for removing paint or varnish it will probably soon get clogged and become blunt. To restore a perfect edge to a scraper demands a knack few amateurs possess. Moreover, the broad, flat blade of the conventional tool is useless in grooves, flutings, carvings and suchlike recesses, especially those found on chairs, etc. A razor-blade is at once too flexible and too brittle and is always a hazard. Use a piece of broken glass. You may think it an amateurish makeshift. We disagree. Antique dealers and cabinet makers use it constantly.

Anyone who went to a primary school remembers the ritual of desk-scraping. Graffiti and ink spots were defenceless against these improvised scrapers.

To ensure making a neat job of it and not scoring the wood, use plenty of bits of glass and throw the old one away as soon as it gets dirty. Use very light pressure. You will soon find that the paint comes off very easily if the angle of attack is right. A few minutes are enough to acquire the knack. The only hazard is 'writer's cramp'; the glass is held between two fingers and fatigue inevitably sets in sooner or later.

After scraping, rub down with the finest grade of glasspaper you can get, leaving the surface absolutely smooth and even. Don't press too hard on the marquetry, you may go right through it, especially if it is loose or has risen (see the section on 'Repairing Marquetry').

Last of all, use steel wool. You can get rolls of it from hardware dealers who specialize in cabinet makers' tools and supplies. Failing this, use ordinary household scouring pads. They produce a fine polish, especially on curves and mouldings.

Veneers and marquetry

Veneering consists of sticking a thin sheet of fine wood over the surfaces of a piece of furniture made of some ordinary timber.

Marquetry consists of decorative or ornamental compositions added to the veneer by inlaying.

These definitions are not superfluous, because there is a tendency to treat the two terms as synonymous.

The complicated technique of veneers and marquetry demands not only special materials but also a manual skill which can be acquired only from good teachers and after much experience.

Our aim is to enable you to repair the commonest kinds of damage or deterioration which disfigure the furniture and simultaneously to attempt to initiate you into development of the art, and to tell you how to recognize the successive periods through which it has passed.

*

Ever since man started using wood for more than immediate, utilitarian purposes, he has contrived to adorn it with incrustations of bone, ivory or horn, and, of course, with other species of wood, which he quickly learnt to differentiate in terms of quality.

André-Charles Boulle is sometimes credited with the invention of both marquetry and veneer. But this is wrong. As early as the sixteenth century and probably before, the Italians had occasionally used the technique. Under Louis XIII, ebony veneers were used on the cabinets for which the fashion had spread to France from Italy and Spain. Nevertheless it was the famous French cabinet maker who was responsible for the triumph of veneer and marquetry. Curiously, André Charles hardly ever used wood in his marquetry: his usual materials were mostly brass and tortoiseshell, sometimes pewter. It is said (and a few examples exist to confirm it) that Boulle always made two of every piece of furniture, and that whatever parts of the marquetry were tortoiseshell in one, were of brass in the other. The explanation of this is that the cutting-out of a marquetry motif was effected in a single operation; a sheet of brass was placed on top of a leaf of tortoiseshell, and because the two materials were cut together the resulting shapes fitted each other perfectly and could be combined in a single inlay. The offcuts from one also fitted the offcuts from the other, but the other way round, so that the ornamentation for the second piece of furniture was automatically to hand. (In English, the two sets are sometimes known as Boulle – or Buhl, which is a corruption – and counter-Boulle.)

*

After Boulle there was a return to a more massive style of furniture, but not for long. In the early eighteenth century, French and English trading companies had been introducing into Europe new species of timber from both East and West Indies. The finest mahogany, called in those days Spanish, came from the West Indies, and there were often satiny and coloured varieties whose advantages cabinet makers were quick to see and exploit. One of the first to do so was Charles Cressent, who appears to have been the originator of the commode as we have since known it. Before him, the commode had been more or less an offshoot of the chest. It can certainly be said that he lightened its forms, gave it longer, slenderer legs and was the first to use those crossbow-shaped bottom rails, *traverses 'en arbalète'*, which are part of the distinctive character of the Régence and Louis XV style.

Here let us pause momentarily and consider what marquetry and veneer consisted of at this period.

Wood for veneering is obtained in either of two ways:

Crosscut consists of cutting a thin, flat film of wood from the seasoned trunk; like a plank but only a few tenths of a millimetre thick, and obviously with its width limited by the diameter of the trunk.

Unrolling, as its name implies, consists of 'unrolling' or 'peeling' a trunk by rotating it about its long axis; the width of the resulting sheet depending on the circumference of the trunk. This is the method now used industrially.

In the eighteenth century, only the first of these two methods was practised. As far as can be seen, high-quality timber was sawn into sheets as thin as the essentially manual nature of the operation permitted. Guessing a little, we may say that unfinished sheets of a thickness of 2 mm were obtained (as compared with 0·4 mm, the usual thickness of veneers today). Planing and sanding would bring the thickness down to about 1·5 mm. This purely technical reason accounts for the fact that genuine eighteenth-century furniture always has thick veneers; even considerably later when the process was developed further, it was impossible to achieve veneers as thin as those which infallibly point to the industrial era.

Curved surfaces were the reason why, in the eighteenth century, veneers had to be as thin as possible. It would have been asking for trouble to try to stick an insufficiently flexible sheet on a convex or concave surface. But though a continual effort was made to reduce the thickness the craftsmen rarely managed to get it below 1·2 mm. Excessive sanding might have produced a lower-quality veneer.

Eighteenth-century veneer, we emphasize once again, *is comparatively thick*. This is an important criterion for the amateur.

Let us now glance at the technique involved in marquetry. As we have seen, André-Charles Boulle cut both background and motifs in a single operation. His method was dropped; his successors' practice was to cut spaces in the background for the motifs, which were prepared separately. This important fact enables one easily to distinguish eighteenth-century work from that of the nineteenth, when improved equipment made it possible to revive Boulle's technique and apply it to veneer.

Slight but perceptible irregularities are, in fact, typical of eighteenth-century marquetry. Joins are more prominent, tiny chisel-marks give evidence of retouching, and asymmetry in the motifs is almost universal.

These little things, which sound unfavourable to the cabinet makers in question, are, on the contrary, just what confers outstanding life and vigour on the marquetry of the period. One recognizes the presence of the craftsman's hand throughout. The perfection of nineteenth-century marquetry, for instance, has an utterly disembodied character, a mindless frigidity totally unrelieved by the different tones of the woods used, well chosen though they are.

This leads us to ask a question which is more important than it sounds; one which promotes our understanding of the forms fashioned by truly creative artists, and the intentions underlying their work. Is there any reason why perfectionism should be the guiding principle of all human endeavour? To discover whether technique is a means, an end or an accessory would not carry us much farther towards an answer. The great creators invented such techniques as would serve their imagination; the opposite process – imagining forms to fit an existing technique – is something which occurs rarely, if at all. A humorous reflection you can sometimes hear from the best restorers on the subject of the cabinet makers of the past, is that 'they didn't make a religion of the plumbline'. Which is true enough; though one should remember that the plumbline is not much used in cabinet making anyway, and that judgement is objectively difficult in connection with furniture which has been subject to the assaults of time, the movement and shrinking of the wood, and normal wear and tear. However, what gave me the answer was not the restorers' observation but something an old craftsman said while I was watching him execute a bit of precision work. I noticed he hardly ever referred to the drawing and commented on this. 'I know,' he said, carrying on with his work meanwhile, 'but then the drawing is just a diagram on the flat. In making a piece of artistic furniture to specification, what matters is *pleasing the eye*.' Surely that is the real perfectionism?

Repairing 'blisters'

'Blisters' are the swellings, large or small in area, which come up in a veneer. They are mainly caused by damp, or by insufficient gluing when the piece was made.

The simplest policy is to try to reheat whatever glue may still exist under the blister, and to apply pressure so that the veneer sticks down again. How is this achieved? Use an electric iron. But proceed with care. If your iron has an adjustable thermostat set the pointer at 'Silk'. If not, guess the temperature as best you can; it does not need to be very high. Protect the veneer with a piece of cardboard or anything else suitable, and apply the iron with a slow movement, using a good deal of pressure. The moment will come when you sense that a slight, tacky adhesion has occurred; this is an indication that the glue has softened. Now let the iron cool down; if necessary, replace it with some heavy object (which, obviously, should be flat). It will be advisable to allow several hours for drying. Failure is always possible, especially if the initial cause was inadequate gluing. In that case, a slit must be made in the blister with a razor blade or a very sharp chisel. Make sure the slit goes *with* the grain, not across it, otherwise the repair will always remain visible. The slit enables you to put in the glue. For preference, use the same kind of glue as the old cabinet makers did: bone glue, melted in the old-fashioned glue-pot with a water-jacket. The best procedure is to press down one side of the blister; this makes the other side come up, so that the slit conveniently gapes open for you to pour in the glue. Then do the other side in the same way, and stroke the area of the mend with your finger so as to squeeze out the superfluous glue. Put the blister under pressure with the help of one or more cramps.

Warning! The piece of wood you put between the cramp and the blister may stick on to the veneer if any more glue comes out of the slit. So put on a sheet of tissue paper first. After drying, it can easily be removed with a fine scraper or a razor blade.

Vinyl glue – and why not?

Bone glue is not commonly sold nowadays; modern cabinet makers use vinyl adhesives, which are more satisfactory from every point of view. There are two methods open to you. The first is to use a vinyl glue instead of the old-fashioned kind, and apply pressure.

The second method is a particularly neat one which does the trick without any special equipment and moreover is easy to control. Work the glue in as above, squeeze out any excess, and leave it to dry for twenty minutes. The next step is to lay tissue paper over the blister and iron it with a warm iron, set at 'Silk'. Press hard for as long as is necessary to ensure adhesion. Then switch off the current to your iron but leave the iron in position; as it gradually cools the glue will do the same, giving perfect adhesion.

And what about neoprene?

Neoprene is a contact adhesive specifically intended for laminates (see the chapter on 'Glues'). As the term implies, mere contact between the two surfaces to be joined, each of which is previously coated with the adhesive, produces perfect adhesion, without pressure. Cabinet makers, however, seem rather slow to welcome it. Is this just traditional conservatism? Anyway, the contact adhesive can be enormously useful to both professional and amateurs, provided *both* surfaces are coated with it. The two things to be stuck – the veneer and the carcase – should both be given a thin, even film of adhesive (use a scraper, or any suitable object with a straight edge, to obtain a smooth covering). Leave them to dry until tacky, so that they no longer stick to you when tested with finger-tip pressure. Then bring the two surfaces together and smooth them over with a piece of board, or any other flat, smooth object. In this way you should be able to achieve an impeccable piece of veneering.

Warning: if you have put on a veneer in this way, never try to take it off again. It's practically impossible. And if you did succeed you would leave a very awkward surface for subsequent veneering.

A method which is sometimes worth trying but is a good deal of a gamble is to use a cork pad. Rub the blister vigorously, with a steady to-and-fro motion, with a cork pad; the heat produced by friction sometimes does the trick. The chief advantage is that the pad cannot damage the varnish.

Cracks

A veneer displaying a network of hair-cracks does not necessarily demand repair; cracks of this kind are just a sign of age. If a piece of veneer has deteriorated so badly that you are compelled to replace it, you may also decide to age it artificially so that its appearance doesn't stick out like a sore thumb. We can give you a few tips for this, but pick whichever method suits your purpose.

Before applying adhesive, thoroughly wet the new piece of veneer. Then iron it with a very hot iron. This sometimes produces tiny cracks and slightly browns the surface.

Hot sand (really hot) has always been an item in the cabinet maker's arsenal. It is used for giving a patina to the background parts of a carving, and for darkening marquetry. Hold the new piece of veneer in something suitable (such as eyebrow tweezers) and dip it in very hot sand, which can be in a saucepan on a gas-ring. Always remember to wet the veneer first, so as to avoid scorching or burning it. Leave it in the sand just long enough and no longer.

Finally, you can seal the grain of the wood (see the section on French polishing), before varnishing with pumice (which is neutral in colour) and with an admixture of umber, which will emphasize the grain of the wood.

Replacing a missing piece

Every case is a special case; hardly ever is a missing fragment merely the equivalent of a lost piece from a jigsaw puzzle. Sometimes a hole has been made by the veneer's being gradually worn away. Sometimes the glue has failed and one day, by mischance, the cleaning duster has torn out a splinter; the fragment was carefully kept for a time, then lost. Or there was an accident; a hard knock, something digging in and tearing the veneer. Or a cigarette burn or the like; or some elusive, quite unexpected cause.

We shall suggest remedies for as many of these special cases as we can.

Holes

We start with these because they are undoubtedly the hardest of the lot. After being sanded and revarnished a few times the veneer wears away, but very unevenly; when a perforation develops it is usually where there is something slightly uneven, such as a blister which was left untreated.

Simply letting in a new piece won't work, because the new veneer, being as yet of its original thickness, would be 'proud' (protruding) and would be practically impossible to reduce to the level of the surrounding surface. Here is the professional craftsman's solution and as far as we know it is the only real answer. You remove the veneer (see the section on this); the area taken off should be two or three times greater than that of the perforation. Trim the edges of the latter a little, not so as to give them sharp, regularly-shaped edges but in order to get rid of any wood that is too thin. Then make a slit along the grain with a razorblade or sharp chisel. By means of this slit, insert a piece of veneer slightly larger than the hole, having first made sure you have chosen a wood whose grain and character are as similar as possible to those of the object under repair.

Centre the piece carefully and fix it down (for example by sticking a needle through it); then, with a pencil, mark the approximate outline of the hole.

Remove the new piece and thin it down gradually from the pencilled line outwards towards the edges, using for this a very sharp wood chisel, glasspaper, a fine file, etc.

Now apply glue and put the piece in position, taking care that all excess glue is removed, and place under pressure. A trick of the trade which cabinet makers find useful is this: between the new piece and the flat piece of wood (really flat and true) which takes the pressure of the cramps, put two or three thicknesses of rubber obtained by cutting up an inner tube. This distributes the pressure evenly and causes it to be applied with a good 'touch'.

When the glue has set, sand carefully to equalize the different thicknesses and achieve a rigorously flat surface.

A final warning! When putting on the new piece, make sure the grain is pointing the right way. A repair with the grain running crossways would be hideous.

Perforated bolls

Burrs or 'bolls' in elm, walnut, cherry and other timbers can be used as veneers to produce original and often beautiful effects, and the great cabinet makers of the eighteenth and nineteenth centuries used them liberally in their finest works. 'Bolls' are, of course, those roughly spherical, knotty extruberances, the result of bad pruning or disease, where proper growth of the tree limb affected has been aborted and has, as it were, turned in on itself. In the sawmill, their fibres are found to lie in swirling, curly, shimmering patterns which have a decided decorative quality. Unfortunately the resulting veneer is somewhat capricious and unreliable. The grain runs in any direction and in many instances contains holes caused by tiny knots, as when a branch began to grow but failed to develop; and by scars, and so on.

When a hole in a veneer is caused by a boll, the trouble has usually developed in the first place from one of these minute knotholes. When the furniture was being made there were probably some which the cabinet maker or polisher was obliged to fill. He is certain to have used shellac. This is easy to buy from firms catering for cabinet makers and such-like; it comes in slabs, like bars of chocolate, in a wide range of shades, from which you can choose the one which suits whatever you are doing. It looks exactly the same when you buy it as it will after being put on; so don't be alarmed at any change in its appearance while you are working with it.

Shellac is comparatively hard and melts when heated. The secret of successful in-filling is to observe a few simple rules. Never melt the shellac over a flame; use a hot bar of iron.

Avoid getting the shellac too hot and making it boil; this will create bubbles, which cause weak points and may show up as holes when it comes to sanding.

Shellac shrinks on cooling, so always use a little more than is necessary. Superfluous shellac, once it has set hard, can be removed with a chisel and then given a perfect surface by sanding.

A missing piece

The policy for this is always the same: treat the problem as one of marquetry. If the piece is regular in shape, you reproduce it as exactly as possible. If it is irregular, try to give it a logical shape (i.e. not just a formless-looking patch); whenever possible, make it something like a parallelogram (*en sifflet*), where what needs mending is a smooth panel (such as a table top or the top of a commode, the front of a drawer, etc.). If an insertion shaped *en sifflet* is not practicable, try to make use of the outer limits of a motif or of a prominently-marked area of grain to effect an 'invisible mend'.

You will inevitably have to remove a certain amount of the old veneer. Depending on the size of the repair, use either a chisel or a very fine-toothed saw (if you possess a veneering saw, so much the better; if not, a small tenon saw will do perfectly). As a guide for the saw you can position a ruler along the line of cut and hold it in place with a couple of cramps. Don't saw deeper than the veneer. A saw-cut in the carcase would create a line of weakness just where you do not want it, along the join. Thoroughly clean off all old glue from the exposed surface of the carcase. Then make a template of the exact shape of the new piece of veneer. For this you will need some thin, stiff cardboard, nicely matching the replacement (if you can, go to a bookbinder for some, it is 0·7 mm thick, very stiff and just right for the job). Make sure your template is perfectly accurate. Before sawing the veneer, use the template to find the best orientation, so as to marry the veins and grain of the new veneer with those of the old to maintain uniformity.

The veneer must be not only sawn flat but forced to remain flat while being sawn; if necessary, cramp it between two pieces of plywood.

Another method, excellent in every way, consists of placing the veneer over the site of the intended repair before trimming the edges of the latter. Then cut both at once; this ensures that, after tidying up any mess left by the old veneer, the new piece will be a perfect fit. (The method does not, however, apply in cases where the outline contains any angles, causing the sawcuts to intersect.)

The cardboard template method is particularly useful in establishing the outlines of pieces missing from a marquetry pattern.

Gluing is carried out along the lines already described. But it should be noted that if the piece of veneer being replaced is large, any surplus glue may produce disastrous results by causing bulges. It is therefore advisable, when cramping-up, to begin at the middle of the new piece, thus forcing the glue outwards and enabling the surplus to come out round the edges.

The thickness of the veneer

Any veneer you can get through ordinary commercial channels is most unlikely to be of the same gauge as the piece requiring replacement because the old veneers and marquetry were substantially thicker than those of our own time. Don't let yourself be discouraged by this irritating problem. In workshops specializing in the restoration of valuable furniture the tiniest offcuts of veneer are saved and hoarded like fine gold, only to prove valueless – the wrong thickness or texture – when it comes to using them.

Here are two ways of getting round the difficulty:

1. *If the difference is minimal*, say between 0·1 and 0·3 mm: before gluing, cut a piece of tissue paper to the necessary shape, saturate it with glue and apply it to the carcase. Let it dry before proceeding to glue up by one of the methods already described. The thickness of the paper, carefully selected for the purpose, will make up the difference. And the resulting repair will be just as

strong, provided that the glue has really penetrated the paper, consolidating its fibres.

2. *If the difference is larger*, simply use two pieces of veneer, one on top of the other. This expedient may bring howls from the purists, but it is indispensable. It will enable you to achieve a high-precision result, because modern veneers are made in several gauges between 0·4 and 0·6 mm. The right combination of these will solve the problem.

Dents in veneer

The cause is always an impact of some kind, usually that of a sharply pointed object: the corner of another piece of furniture, or a crate carelessly handled by removers' men, or a marble sculpture whose position had to be altered, or the projecting angle of a wall. Repairing dents is a trying business; there is no single, simple answer. Sometimes the damage, on examination, proves to be slight: the veneer is a bit crunched but the carcase is intact.

The dent can be eliminated by applying steam; this makes the fibres of the wood swell up and resume their proper position. Take a piece of rag of just sufficient size to cover the damaged area, soak it well, and place it in position. Apply a really hot iron, so as to produce a copious amount of steam. Don't keep it there too long: the aim is to penetrate *only the surface* of the wood, without affecting the glue or spoiling the varnish. Repeat several times. You will see the wood recovering its original shape, which it will retain after drying out.

A harder blow, denting not only the veneer but also the carcase, is more serious. You will find that the forcible bending of the veneer has broken it across. Using a very thin tool detach the damaged part of the veneer and fold it back a little way; you will probably have to split it along the grain. Any pieces that break right off should be carefully saved if they look usable. The carcase, usually made of softwood like pine or poplar, will be deeply marked.

The simplest solution is to use plastic wood, obtainable until recently only in tins but now also available in tubes. Plastic wood, which is a soft, pliable paste, must be allowed to dry out very thoroughly before the veneer is put back on. The solvent used in plastic wood is alcohol in some brands, acetone in others; it must have time to evaporate completely if it is not to cause trouble after gluing. Apply the plastic wood with a spatula or palette knife. If you find it has cracked or shrunk during drying, put on some more and allow that to dry out too. After that you can sand or rasp it, just like ordinary wood.

A quicker method is to use shellac. Directions for this have already been given: heat it with a hot bar of iron, never over a naked flame. The veneer can then be glued on to this new support, which should first have been made perfectly smooth. The repair will probably have to be completed by sanding and revarnishing.

A split in the carcase

Damage of this severity may well demand more repairing than the amateur's skill and tools will run to. But, briefly, the whole of the veneer on the split panel has to be removed so that the causes of the split can then be investigated; this implies a deep knowledge of wood, especially as the veneer, despite having given way to some extent, has nevertheless curbed the movement of the split portion of the carcase, which may, therefore, produce further movement. What is the correct solution? To close the split by inserting thin fillets secured by glue? To strengthen the panel by small cross-pieces at the back (a method also much used in repairing paintings on wood panels that have split)? Some cabinet makers favour canvas straps, glued on, to hold the panel together. And a point which must always be reckoned with is that the split may have been caused by deformation in the whole structure, in which case general reconstruction will be necessary.

There are some things it is always better to hand over to the expert.

Replacing veneer on a round or convex support

A contact adhesive is best in cases of this kind; it avoids the use of cramps on round or convex places in a piece of furniture. Special problems like this are only to be solved by using a special substance, correctly applied. However, here are a few tricks of the trade which may help you too.

The plaster mould method

This means using plaster of Paris, not as an adhesive but to make a mould which exactly copies the contours of the piece of veneer to be stuck on. This constitutes a former which holds the new veneer in place with absolute precision. Mix your plaster in the normal way (remember: add plaster to water, not water to plaster). When you sense that the plaster has begun 'working', apply it to the part to be reproduced (if you like, mix some plumber's tow with the plaster first; this makes it less elusive to handle and also acts as an armature to hold it together while it is setting). As soon as the mould has set hard, which takes only a few minutes, remove it and put it aside to dry.

The sandbag method

This is by far the easiest method of all. You make a flat bag, only a little larger than the piece of veneer to be pressed on. Fill the bag with sand (until recently, it was custom to heat the sand first so as to soften the bone glue then used). Put a flat piece of wood on top and apply pressure with cramps or weights. The sand moulds itself to the convex surface and distributes the pressure evenly.

The strap method

This is a time-honoured method which you may find useful, particularly on round components (such as the feet of some pieces of furniture, though as a rule these are not veneered). It consists simply of tightly binding the part in question with a woven strap. The strap is well wetted first, so that it stretches and is thoroughly supple. When the buckle is done up the strap is drawn tight and exerts strong pressure. Incidentally, some of the straps now available, made of synthetics, have special buckles on the wire-strainer principle, which exert high tension.

Removing veneer

We have said plenty about *sticking* – how to glue a piece of veneer on. But what about *unsticking* – taking a piece of veneer off? There are some repair jobs in which it is essential.

The old-fashioned glues present no great difficulty and respond to heat and humidity. Use a dishcloth and a hot iron, taking care to wet the cloth as often as may be necessary. Everyone has his own pet method for speeding the result. Some recommend a pinch of bicarbonate of soda or washing soda in the water; others, a well-stirred mixture of alcohol and hot water (in which case the cloth and hot iron are not required). All these recipes are effective.

Modern glues present a more complex problem.

Vinyl adhesives can be softened by heat, using an electric iron set at 'Silk'. But mechanical help is also necessary. Have a suitable flat tool ready to hand, which can be inserted under the veneer to prise it up as the glue softens. Contact adhesives also react to heat but are most sensitive to solvents, such as acetone, benzine, benzoline, trichloroethylene, etc.

The chain method of ageing

One form of damage found in veneered furniture is an indication that the work is faked; the damage was added to make it look genuine. Light blows have been inflicted, leaving marks about the size and shape of a grain of rice. Their uniformity, and the fact that they make the wood darker than the rest, render them easily recognizable. This practice is sometimes known in the trade as thrashing. The faker uses a length of ordinary chain and thrashes the piece with it, more or less at random but particularly on sharp edges, the resulting marks being just what you might expect a chain to produce. A little common sense and alertness will suffice to arouse your suspicions. A similar effect can be obtained by tapping with the flat end of a hammer.

Bands and other brass ornamentation

Furniture is sometimes embellished with brass ornamentation, emphasizing the general lines of the design. Some of these are bands fitting snugly in half-round grooves on the legs of a table, or, occasionally, the uprights, glazing bars or applied mouldings of a glazed cabinet.

It is most irritating when these ornaments loosen in the course of time, especially as they are not easy to stick back in place. Worse still is the nightmare of having to replace those that are lost.

Let us take first the ornaments that are neither broken nor distorted but have simply come off.

If you have a small soldering iron of the kind used by electricians, you can use it to heat the brass strip before pressing it firmly back into its groove. The heat will soften the glue and fix the ornament in place. Another method you can try is to make the head of a hammer really hot (but take care not to burn the handle).

If these methods fail, try to clean off the old glue on the strip with a file, keeping the strip flat on a true surface while doing so. The groove can be cleaned out with a tiny flat chisel or mortise chisel (these can be bought in sizes from 2 mm upwards). Then use a contact adhesive on both surfaces.

Brass strips which are twisted, broken or stretched must be replaced with new ones. Shops which specialize in materials of this kind sell them by the yard. You may be able to fix them yourself, following the directions given here, but in most cases you will do better to take the job to a qualified craftsman. Attaching brass strips, bands and ornamental mouldings requires a skill born of many years' practice.

Giving furniture the right patina

What sort of surface do you like?

There are some words we use so often that we forget what they really mean. People blithely confuse patina with dirt; a dangerous error. The fact is that the shining film which gives rustic charm to some piece of furniture discovered in a farmyard may well prove disappointing when transferred to another settting; even, when strongly lit, somewhat repellent. And the dull, opaque coating hastily brushed on by a junk dealer has nothing in common with the slow ripening which only time can give. In any case, different woods have their own ways of ageing. Oak and walnut are capable of actually losing their pigmentation over a period of time. Most Gothic furniture – if genuine – is pale, hardly even golden. Beech changes colour little or not at all; the reddest cherry-wood turns blond; elm and chestnut darken slightly, especially in the soft parts between the grain; so does ash, though its tendency to deviate from its original colour is on the whole very slight. The true pale honey colour of the best pieces of mahogany furniture is only achieved by years of hand polishing.

All of which is a long way from the kind of patina which can be put on with a brush!

A patina is a caress. A caress for the sense of sight, which discovers the true contours of a piece of furniture and sees their saliences reinforced by subtle differentiations not of colour but of light. And a caress for the sense of touch. No faking, no sanding or artificial signs of wear can ever take the place of the polished smoothness created by long use. A genuine antique piece can be stripped with powerful chemicals, washed, thoroughly rinsed and allowed to dry, and will immediately regain its shine at the touch of your rag or cloth without needing any wax or other polishing material at all.

All you have done is to restore the effect of long years of care, the maintenance patiently applied by generations of devoted, loving ownership.

It is true that many pieces, when new, were given a coat of stain to bring out the inherent decorative qualities of the material. But the stain used was a decoction of vegetable origin, in other words made with water; hence it penetrated the wood only for a short distance. It was utterly different from the atrocious brews daubed on with such frenzy by professional prettifiers. After staining came polishing – with beeswax, that golden natural substance which, in time, builds up a translucent deposit for which there is no substitute.

However, we do sometimes find ourselves compelled to reconstitute a patina which has been destroyed by neglect or by exposing furniture to the weather, or to harmonize restored portions with the whole. Various products are available for the purpose and it is not for us to discuss their relative merits. Some of them are combined stains and polishes. Our own advice, given below, is to use natural methods, though we also suggest ways for accelerating the effects which are normally created only by the lapse of time.

Hot waxing

The first treatment to give to a piece of furniture, after cleaning or stripping it, is a coat of liquid wax. You can either use one of the high-quality standard brands of furniture polish, diluted with turpentine, or mix your own by melting a cake of beeswax in a water-jacket and adding turpentine, stirring continuously meanwhile. The right proportion is 250 grammes of beeswax to 1 litre of turpentine. Be careful not to let the liquid catch fire; have a lid ready to extinguish a flare-up if it occurs.

The diluted wax is applied with an ordinary brush, care being taken to cover every detail. The aim of this initial operation is to nourish the pores of the wood, which will have been scoured empty by cleaning.

Leave the work to dry out thoroughly. Absorption will be total. The piece is then ready to undergo the highly important operation of hot waxing.

Arm yourself with a cake of wax, a brazing torch or blowlamp with a flat (fishtail) burner, and a suitable brush or two. You will soon acquire the requisite knack.

Soften the wax slightly and rub it on the wood, rapidly but with plenty of pressure. You will find that a little wax is deposited on the surface by each movement to and fro. Pass the flame of your torch over these deposits. They will melt, sink deeply into the wood, close the pores and spread out over the surface. If there is too little wax anywhere you simply put on more and run over it with the flame – carefully, of course, so as to avoid blackening the wood or setting the wax alight. If there is too much wax anywhere it is easily removed by energetic polishing with a stiff brush; not having had time to harden completely, it comes off easily. Undiluted wax dries quickly and the brush eliminates any irregularities; a brilliant surface appears at once. On carvings and mouldings, use a burnisher – and don't be frightened off by this technical term, the tool is one you can easily make yourself. Take a small piece of hardwood and cut one end of it to a sharp bevel edge. With this you can scrape the protuberant details without fear of damage, such as a metal tool would certainly inflict.

You have now made the wax sink well into the wood, impregnating it for keeps. Maintenance is no trouble; an occasional rub with a soft rag or woollen duster restores the brilliance.

Some cabinet makers use a hot iron instead of a blowlamp. This avoids the risk of scorching and darkening the wood, but we find it makes the wax go too runny so that all of it sinks into the wood instead of sealing the superficial pores correctly. Here again, touch is all.

There is another method which produces a high gloss, but which, in our opinion, is rather artificial. It consists of using a liquid wax and following it up with a coat of copal varnish dissolved in alcohol. This is more akin to French polishing than to hot waxing.

There are plenty of recipes for 'miracle' polishes. One of them is a mixture of stearine or spermaceti with beeswax; paraffin (kerosene) wax is also sometimes used. Many excellent polishes are now available commercially, based on highly successful formulae whose ingredients include very hard vegetable waxes which, when dry, give a tough durable finish; examples are 'carnauba' wax from South America, and wax extracted from palm leaves.

Shoe polish

Though comparatively expensive, shoe polish has always been one of the cabinet maker's most valuable allies. It is used for heightening the details of carvings. Coloured polish, not the transparent neutral kind, is of course what you want. You put it on with a small brush (this provides your discarded toothbrush with a second career). Leave the polish to dry for a few hours, then rub the carving with a stiff brush or wooden burnisher; the parts in relief turn lighter, the undercuts will stay dark because the brush or burnisher can't reach them.

In France, one famous manufacturer of shoe polish has brought out an excellent product designed specially for cabinet makers, suitably coloured for different varieties of wood.

Mechanical aids

In recent years the accessories available for use with portable electric drills have included a polisher, usually made of lamb's wool. In practice this produces rather disappointing results, although in principle it looks like a sound method for obtaining in a minute or two the effect of decades of maintenance by hand. The cause is a simple one: portable electric drills run at 2500 r.p.m. or even more; some of the two-speed drills run at 1400 and 900 r.p.m. At speeds like these the wax melts and is dispersed by centrifugal force. Even the varnishes in normal use disintegrate because the friction generates more heat than they can stand. So it is no use expecting to polish a piece of furniture by this means. However, a special mechanical polisher has been designed and put on the market; it works on the same principle but runs at only 400–500 r.p.m., the threshold beyond which the wax breaks down. The polishing attachments provided are either brushes of different degrees of stiffness, or a sheepskin roller. Another item of equipment, which deserves to be better known than at present, is a disc made from a material directly derived from that of which scouring cloths are made. These discs are invaluable. Although their action is gentle they are just as effective on wood, which they polish to perfection, as on bronze or iron.

A restoration carried out with new wood can be given an exemplary patina after treatment with these discs, which are available in various grades to provide different degrees of abrasion. The same discs can also be used for straightforward cleaning; handled judiciously, at a speed from 500 to 1000 r.p.m., they leave the wood clean without making circular grooves or scratches.

Special cases

All the woods commonly used in cabinet making, such as oak, walnut and wild cherry and other fruitwoods, can be treated in the manner described here. So can mahogany, although most people prefer it varnished.

Cuban mahogany, which is very dense in texture, gains nothing from being hot-waxed; the same applies to South American rosewood, ebony and lignum vitae. These are outstandingly hard, close-grained woods, which are virtually without pores to be sealed.

Teak, at one time used exclusively for exotic furniture, has been domesticated into household use by the talent of Swedish designers. It is a wood whose oily texture protects it from deterioration, so that it practically looks after itself. If it ever does need cleaning, use plenty of trichlorethylene on a clean rag.

When it has dried, use teak oil, a special liquid far more suitable than wax. After that, rub with a duster in the ordinary way.

Resinous woods
These take very kindly to hot waxing and equally so to an under-coat of wax and turpentine, with which, of course, they have a natural affinity. However, there is a time-honoured recipe which has been used ever since the early Middle Ages and which can be recommended on several counts; its results are remarkable. This is *linseed oil*. Use it as hot as you can and go on applying it until the wood rejects it, that is to say until you can see the oil staying on the surface instead of sinking in. Let it become part-way dry, then wipe off the excess and leave until drying is complete; this will take several days, even in hot, dry weather. This is the only drawback with linseed oil.

The final step is to polish with a brush or cloth producing a bright, lasting shine. A considerable advantage is that even the softest wood is made perceptibly harder by being impregnated with linseed oil, which is therefore suitable not only for resinous woods, but also for poplar and lime, which are rather sad and colourless in themselves but, after treatment, display a delightful golden radiance.

Local customs

Certain county and regional practices were effectively used in the preparation of timber – oak particularly – for what, in early times, amounted to joinery in the contriving of simple furniture such as joint stools, refectory tables, cupboards, benches and the like, either to be left plain or more or less decorated with hand carving, depending on the status of the family requiring it.

In modern times, the householder is rightly terrified of damp which, once established in the soft timbers of roof or flooring, can destroy the value of his house in a very few years. Some of the practices outlined below may therefore come as a shock, though it must be borne in mind that the methods used were for curing oak and not soft woods.

For centuries, oak was seasoned by immersion in water. After felling and barking, the trunks were trundled into ponds or meres and left there for long periods of time. This practice is said to have originated in Flanders, and Flemish craftsmen frequently used such timber in cabinet making.

Of course, one suspects that not just any old pond or mere was used and that knowledge of those ponds whose waters were rich in mineral salts had been handed down by tradition.

An amusing story comes to us from Burgundy (which was not so remote from Flanders as might appear: that province was part of the empire of Charles the Bold). The accounts of the abbot who commissioned the building of the Hôtel-Dieu at Tonnerre (Yonne) record the abbot's own justification of his outlay for the timber frame. He says, in effect: 'I wavered long between two lots of timber. The first had been seasoned for only (only!) five hundred years; the other, for six hundred. It was dearer, but more suitable for serious building.'

It is astonishing to realize that, in the fifteenth century, timber was being used which dated from the time of Charlemagne. Contemporary documents make it clear that seasoning consisted of prolonged immersion; so long, in fact, that the oak became as if petrified.

In Brittany, as in coastal areas of the British Isles, immersion was widely practised, but with a significant difference. The trunks were cast into the sea, and we know beyond doubt that it was the custom to bury them deep in the mud. This was a time-honoured procedure. It has always been known that wood rots only in the air. Underwater or buried in mud, it loses its sap, is penetrated by mineral salts and undergoes a transformation not unlike petrification. In Brittany, there are thousands of old cottages whose roofs, supported by old ships' timbers, have remained sound for hundred of years. Such timbers are often so hard that it is impossible to drive a nail into them. To this day, much Breton furniture is made from wood which has spent some time in the sea. Not long ago, we saw an old cabinet maker burying in the sand of the seashore the components of a piece of furniture he had just made: he told us it would stay there for about a year. Well, he knew what he was doing.

A tip well known to cabinet makers is that when you have to

use a piece of new wood in restoring an old piece of furniture, you can make quite sure of its not warping by soaking it in brine for a week. Presumably it has to be thoroughly rinsed on being taken out, otherwise an unwelcome efflorescence of salt crystals would appear later on its surface.

Woods which have been water-seasoned can be recognized by certain peculiarities. Oxides from the water, and tannin in the oak itself, combine to colour the oak very strongly, right to the heart. Another characteristic is that the wood is hardly ever a prey to woodworm and other pests. In a few cases they may manage to penetrate soft places, especially in the sapwood, if any of it has been left (usually it has not). Finally, these timbers pass the cabinet maker's acid test: when he planes them they yield no shavings; the blade removes a cloud of short, broken fibres.

Death to stains!

The most precious piece of furniture can be disfigured by ordinary carelessness: a wet glass, an upset inkpot, spilt perfume, grease, a cigarette burn. The blemish becomes a perpetual reproach, you see only it and not the cherished furniture itself. However, the case is never hopeless; the most unsightly stain can be conquered.

Stains from damp

The base of a glass or vase or the bottom of a bottle leaves a white ring on a polished surface. This is not a serious matter in cases where contact was reasonably brief. Let the mark dry thoroughly, then rub with plenty of turpentine, letting it soak in, and apply fresh polish. If this fails, which it sometimes does on woods that are light in colour, rub in a pat of butter until it is completely absorbed.

On stained furniture (i.e. those that have been given a coat of stain), the wetness removes the pigment. The only thing to do is to give the affected part a new coat of stain. If this scares you, try wetting the whole of the surface of the piece with a sponge dipped in a mixture of strong detergent and water (one or two small teaspoonsful, say, to a litre of water); this slightly lightens the colour of the whole and may make it homogeneous.

Alcohol

Glasses put down carelessly on your furniture are the main source of this, but it can also come from a bottle being upset, or scent, medicine and so on getting split. On polished surfaces alcohol leaves a mark like that of ordinary wetness, and the treatment is the same. But the damage is decidedly worse on varnished furniture, because most of the varnishes in common use are soluble in alcohol. Light sanding with tissue paper (very fine glasspaper) is the first step; then build up the surface again (see the chapter on 'French polishing').

Grease, fats and oils

Whether the marks they make are only on the surface or sink in deeply, fatty or oily substances, animal, vegetable or mineral in origin, sometimes pose annoying problems. In theory, benzoline will cope with them, and so will benzine and trichlorethylene; when all else fails, highly refined cigarette-lighter fuel will succeed; ether, too, is highly effective except when the mark goes deep in, in which case it is too volatile.

The drawback of solvents is that they attack glue and loosen veneer. But on any furniture not veneered they work like a charm.

Another very effective method, with the advantage of being harmless to marquetry and veneer, is to use talc. Spread a thick layer of it on the spot and warm it very gently with a hot iron protected by several thicknesses of tissue paper. Both the talc and the paper will soak up the grease. Start again with a fresh lot of talc and paper, and repeat until the spot disappears. Fuller's earth can be used instead of talc.

In some cases where a piece of furniture has perhaps been used as a bench, and is disfigured by oily swarf having fallen on it, the methods just described will answer very well, but only in the second stage of rehabilitation. The first stage consists of loosening the oil marks by applying some other kind of oily or greasy substance, appropriately chosen, and rubbing it in; this may succeed in removing the marks, and can then itself be removed, as directed above.

Ink

There are numbers of recipes for removing ink spots from furniture, which is in itself an indication that the problem has never really been solved. We have got no further with it today than people had done a hundred years ago; with this difference, that ink is no longer much used, even by schoolchildren.

So we are more often challenged by old ink stains, on bureaux, tables, secretaires and the like, than by recent ones.

Here are a few methods which undoubtedly work but which may be defeated by one kind of ink or another; so you may have to try each in turn.

A fresh ink stain
Wash with water, then use lemon juice.

An old ink stain
First sand lightly to get rid of extraneous substances and expose the surface of the wood. Place a cottonwool pad over the stain and pour sulphuric acid on to the pad – this prevents the acid from running about; after two or three minutes, inspect for results to see whether you are on the right track. Repeat with a fresh pad. Not many inks can withstand sulphuric acid, which possesses the advantage of not damaging the wood.

Oxalic acid, diluted with warm water, is also highly effective; so is muriatic acid, that well-known household specific.

Inks used to be made from 'oak apples' (oak galls, also known as nut galls), ferrous sulphate, copper sulphate and a decoction of logwood. When steel nibs came in and quill pens went out, the copper sulphate, which corroded the nibs, was omitted, but otherwise the recipe stayed much as before. It contains no ingredient which is not easily conquered with one or another of the acids now in common use and easy to obtain.

Red ink is often more recalcitrant. It is essentially vegetable in composition, being made of an infusion of wood from a species of Brazilian tree (*Caesalpina echinata*) in vinegar, *plus* madder, indigo (from the seventeenth to the nineteenth century), alum and gum arabic. Oxalic acid, well diluted with warm water, is the answer. Or muriatic acid can be used instead, heavily diluted with warm water to which a few drops of hydrogen peroxide have been added. When treating a really old red ink stain you may see it turn dark, even black, but don't worry: carry on, the treatment does work.

If you can find a chemist or drugstore willing to supply you with potassium hyperchlorate, you can use it in the same way as the specifics mentioned, heavily diluted with warm water.

Wine

Wine, like fruit juices, can make peculiarly tenacious stains on wood. However, they hardly ever go very deep. Clean the surface by light scraping or sanding, then use muriatic acid diluted with lukewarm water. While the area is still wet with acid, put a few drops of hydrogen peroxide (see page 6) on it.

Sulphur fumes readily decompose the pigments in wine and those in any fruit juice or vegetable sap. But exposing the affected part of a piece of furniture to these fumes is an awkward business. Place a saucer beside the stain, with a stiff piece of cardboard under it to insulate the wood against heat, and burn some bits of sulphur candle of the kind used for purifying barrels, hogsheads, etc. The fumes will rise vertically; now place a paper cone, like a dunce's cap, or, even better, the lid of a cheese dish, over the stain and the saucer. The fumes will completely fill this confined space and 'bathe' the surface of the wood.

Blood

This is a more frequent cause of stains than might be thought. It is the origin of some of the otherwise unaccountable stigmata that one finds on furniture which has been through a long career of vicissitudes.

Bloodstains are easy to take out with ordinary hydrogen peroxide (see page 6). If the stain proves stubborn, ask your chemist or drugstore for some sodium thiosulphate diluted to 5 per cent. Dab the stain with it, in the confidence of ultimate victory.

Burns

These are wounds, not stains. No natural or artificial chemical can ever remove the discoloration of wood that has been burnt by a hot iron carelessly put down, or a forgotten cigarette or cigar. Only by deep scraping or sanding can such marks be mitigated or removed.

French polishing

To give a permanent lustrous coat to a whitewood piece, or to obliterate scratches and grazes from a valuable antique commode, demands a certain basic knowledge combined with the manual skill we associate with the lifelong craftsmen.

However, modern preparations are continually tending to facilitate the work of both the professional and the amateur. It is now possible to say that french polishing is something anyone can do, with the sole reservation that there is no one universal answer: every case must be studied on its merits and treated accordingly. We shall try to show how to do this.

Brief review of the varnishes now available

One needs to acquaint oneself with the characteristics both of the traditional and of the most modern varnishes, so as to know exactly how to apply them and, what is equally important, which is the right one for a given job. Hence this rapid review.

Oil-based varnishes

We are including these merely for completeness; they are not applied with a pad, which is the 'French' polisher's primary tool. They consist of copal resin boiled up with linseed oil or imported oils. The nature of the ingredients makes them slow to dry, but the final result is usually very good provided every coat is allowed to dry out thoroughly before the next is put on. Note that they cannot be thinned with alcohol, but with turpentine (if natural turpentine is not to hand, you can, at a pinch, use white spirit, which is synthetic turpentine; but never mix turpentine and white spirit).

It is possible by means of these oil-based varnishes to build up a good foundation for french polishing, but is it really desirable to mix two techniques in this way? Whenever using a varnish of this type it is essential to remove any traces of oil or grease from the surface of the wood, otherwise the varnish does not 'take' securely; a preliminary washing-down with petrol or trichlorethylene is always advisable. By sanding carefully with pumice powder between coats – lightly after the first, more vigorously after the second – an effect exactly like french polishing can be obtained.

Cellulose varnishes

These are the commonest kind. They consist chiefly of shellac and cellulose dissolved in alcohol and are the most popular because of their remarkable transparency and ease of application. They are very hard. The only snag is to avoid using them on any wood you suspect of being less than perfectly dry.

One of the advantages of a cellulose varnish is that it dries quickly, making it possible to complete the job in a short time, without much delay between coats.

Alkyd varnishes

These are very tough and durable but have the disadvantage of drying slowly, which makes them vulnerable to airborne dust. However, they also possess undeniable advantages. They play no part in french polishing but are so widely used today that we cannot omit them here. They are put on with a brush, and as their consistency is usually fairly thick it is advisable to draw out each coat as thin as possible and put one coat crosswise over another, avoiding runs and 'fat edges'. Thorough sanding with glasspaper after every coat is essential. Or flower paper, which should be wetted first, can be used.

'Plastic' varnishes

All these have a tremendous future: the epoxy resins, polyesters and polyurethanes, the ureaformaldehyde and phenolic resins and so on. As a rule they are presented as two separate substances, the plastic varnish itself and a catalyst, the hardener.

The only 'plastic' varnishes which are relevant here are the polyesters. They supersede all the traditional methods of varnishing furniture. Advantages, aesthetic as well as practical, outstrip everything previously known. Finally, they completely cut out the conventional preliminaries such as sanding, sealing and so on. They are put on with a gun, and for this reason are perhaps outside the range of the genuine amateur. To achieve perfect results one needs the proper equipment, sufficient experience to acquire the delicate knack of using the gun and, finally, a dust-free work space.

And now, what about french polishing?

This quick run-down on the current varnishes brings us to the main subject of this section: 'french' polishing, the pillar of traditional cabinet making.

The basic ingredients are of the simplest: copal, shellac and other imported resins, dissolved in spirit (alcohol). Of course everyone has his own way of making them up, some special additional substance which he claims is an improvement on the original mixture. You should perhaps take care to get special varnishing spirit, which is obtainable from any specialized merchant, rather than methylated spirit, which can be bought from most hardware stores, chemists and so on. In fact, though the latter is quite safe to use, people say the adulterant added to it spoils the varnish; but don't worry about this, it is one of those professional fads which have more to do with ancient tradition than contemporary fact.

What *is* french polishing?

In principle, french polishing is a technique of varnishing in which a cloth pad is used instead of a brush.

The pad does various things which no brush could ever do. It acts as a reservoir of varnish, enabling a whole surface to be treated without stopping to refill. It regulates the release of varnish, avoiding the runs and fat edges which are the varnisher's bugbear. It is a direct extension of the hand, sensitively transmitting the subtlest variations of touch. Its fibres keep the varnish evenly mixed and the ingredients do not separate out. Finally, it serves not only for varnishing but also for polishing, and for the preliminary sealing of the pores of the wood with powdered pumice, which it withholds or releases automatically, as the surface may require.

Making a pad

The pad should always be of the shape and size of a nice, large egg. Vary its volume to suit your own hand if you like, but that is all.

You will need two pads.

The *first* should be *fairly coarse*, for sealing the grain. A piece of fine hessian filled with rags of various kinds will do. Always take care to see that the rags are clean and colourfast. We cannot make this warning too strongly: *the spirit your pad soaks up may loosen any dye in the rags and make stains on the wood*.

The *second* should be *finer* in texture and very supple. Cotton jersey or mutton cloth is ideal provided it is not new, in which case it will shed bits of fluff. An old jersey and old knitted underwear (not of the cellular or string vest type) are excellent.

The stuffing of these pads should be other kinds of highly absorbent rags with plenty of spring in them, such as knitted woollens, shoddy or woollen rags. White cotton waste, which is easy to buy, is suitable. The outer cover of an egg shaped pad requires a piece of fabric no larger than from 12 to 15 cm square. But you will have to use twice as much because, in order always to be working with a clean pad, you will constantly need to turn the outer cover inside out. So make sure the cover is large enough.

Preliminary operations

Never start french polishing before making the surface of the wood absolutely smooth. The first operation is always thorough sanding, using finer and finer glasspaper and working with the grain, not across it. After this, remove all traces of dust and look along the wood at eye level to make sure it really is smooth.

Another essential is to work in a warm room, at 15–16 °C. At higher temperatures (20 °C) the spirit evaporates too fast.

Sealing the grain

Most species of wood have tiny hollow veins, known aptly enough as 'pores', which are in fact the medullary canals through which the sap of the tree circulates. These 'pores' are more or less marked in different species. It is essential to close them. If the wood is painted they are simply covered up. But in varnishing (which is what french polishing really is) we cannot do this, since the objective is precisely to bring out the decorative beauty of the wood. So we use pumice powder. This is available at low cost from specialized merchants; but you may find that in particularly delicate work you cannot use it as it is but must sift it through a fine sieve.

The medium which is to carry the powder is spirit (alcohol). Soak your pad in this. Then dip it in the pumice powder and coat the surface of your work with the mixture, using small circular movements at the start and gradually increasing the radius so that each movement covers as much of the surface as possible. In this way you go over the grain *in every direction*. To avoid accentuating the pores, don't bear down on the pad; the operation of filling them is not intended to result in a renewed sanding. Shake out your pad as soon as it gets dirty; do not let it become encrusted.

And don't overdo the spirit; if you use too much it will soak into the wood, loosen the veneer (if any) and cause swelling, followed by shrinking, thus jeopardizing smoothness. To make the pumice powder hold well, add a few drops of polish (see below) to your pad as soon as you have acquired the knack of the correct movement. But take care not to use too much. French polishing is an *art of moderation*.

Squint along your work, as you did after sanding it, to check results. The moment will come when filling seems complete: a smooth surface meets your gaze. Pause for a few minutes while the work dries. After a while you will see that some degree of shrinking has occurred: the pores are showing again, though less prominently. You must repeat the filling operation, but already you can use a more liberal allowance of polish.

It is important not to polish continuously, and to disregard the impression of instantaneous drying-out produced by the evaporation of the spirit. With a little patience you will see that your polish is 'working', as craftsmen say. That lovely, glassy surface you thought you had achieved is no longer so perfect, it needs several hours in which to dry.

Polishing is performed with a constant mixture of 50 per cent varnish to 50 per cent spirit. It is out of the question for you to make up your own polishes, as is done by professional cabinet makers who have been in the trade all their lives. Nor should you try to choose a varnish yourself from among the various makes on the market. Get advice from someone who really knows. All you have to tell him is what kind of wood you are working on and what effect you are aiming for; he will recommend the appropriate brand.

Mix your varnish and spirit in a bottle and shake it well every time you put some on to your pad. Having dampened the pad with the polish – never excessively – apply it to the wood in a series of more or less elongated figure-8 movements. Examine your work against the light to make sure that you have gone evenly everywhere, without runs or patches. Work with a light hand. Never let the pad get soiled with dust, pumice powder or anything else. Turn the outer cover over from time to time, so as always to work with a clean pad.

Every pass with the pad leaves a thin film of polish, i.e. dilute varnish, and the instantaneous evaporation of the spirit immediately produces a dry surface. By making several passes in succession you can progressively add to this film. But stop in time to give the polish a chance to dry out properly, in depth.

When it has done so you will discover flaws: places where the varnish has sunk, built up too thickly, or contracted into wrinkles. The remedy is buffing – virtually a combination of sanding and polishing. There are various methods of buffing; the simplest is to use flower paper (sometimes known as 'wet and dry') wetted with water; but the best answer is to use the finest grade of flower paper obtainable, with a little vaseline instead of water. You can use a sanding pad, but take care it is not too soft and supple, otherwise it may catch on the rough places and raise the surface instead of reducing it. This is impossible with something harder, such as a cork pad; better still is a wooden block with bevelled edges.

Before you carry on again with your polishing, clean the work carefully to remove any dust or lubricant left after buffing. Thorough wiping may be enough, but it will do no harm to go one better and polish the surface with a chamois leather or a sponge – a natural sponge, *not* a plastic one.

Continue applying polish as before, and if necessary, buff again after the second coat. The great essential, if you want first class results, is to let your work dry thoroughly every time.

Finally, after a twenty-four hours' drying period, you can finish off the job.

This is a very simple process but demands a delicate touch. With a perfectly clean pad of very closely woven stuff, dipped in spirit alone (special finishing spirit is obtainable), go over your work for the last time, *very* quickly and lightly, using figure-8 movements at first and straight passes forwards and backwards to finish off. The object of the final movement is to impart the ultimate perfect gloss. The unmixed spirit must not be given time to dissolve and soften the dry polish but should just coat the surface, so that, on drying, the polish is perfectly equalized and shows no traces of the movements of the pad. When drying is complete, you can if you wish polish the work with a chamois leather wetted with a very little of your polish mixture, taking care not to shake or stir it this time, so that the varnish at the bottom, which is very slightly abrasive, does not mingle with the liquid on top.

A time-saving method

New products are continually cutting down long, tiresome processes and difficult, skilled operations. Sealing the grain with pumice powder, which is the key to successful french polishing, can now be by-passed by using a *hard base*, a ready-made liquid seal; followed by careful sanding, this produces a fairly good result. It is fair to add that products such as this are always being improved, and it will not be long before they entirely supersede the conventional methods. On the foundation provided by a liquid seal the polish can be successfully built up either with a pad or with a brush; in the latter case the polish will be one of the alkyd varnishes, whose consistency renders them self-equalizing – they spread out smoothly of their own accord after application, and hardly shrink at all in drying.

Special problems: a few hints
Stained wood or stained polish?
The beauty of french polishing lies mainly in its transparency, hence it should be as nearly as possible colourless. Tinted polishes

should be used with great caution. It is much better to stain the wood to the desired shade before polishing. The stains available for the purpose are either water stains or spirit stains.

Water stains are made either of a natural colouring agent, vegetable or mineral in origin, or else of aniline (a coal-tar extract), dissolved in water.

If the shade you want can be achieved with a natural colouring agent, such as walnut juice or logwood, you can be quite sure of getting a fast colour, whereas some of the aniline colours are sensitive to ultra-violet light.

Spirit stains are usually made from aniline.

Water stains take a certain time to dry and have the drawback of bringing up the grain. You will therefore have to sand *after* staining, which of course may alter the colour a bit so that you have to put on more stain. At the same time, sanding after staining has the advantage of emphasizing the decorative quality of the grain.

Spirit stains dry almost instantly, so that you do not have to wait long before polishing. The only risk is that the colour may deteriorate if the piece is continually exposed to sunlight.

Colouring agents are being improved all the time, and some makes bear the word 'Permanent' on the container, meaning that they do not react to light.

Scratches on french polish

The polish must be renewed over the affected area. Everything depends on the seriousness of the damage. To treat an ordinary scratch, sand lightly to equalize the surface and try to soften the old polish with spirit. If it dissolves and goes tacky, spread it out with a pad on which you have placed a little fresh polish. Proceed exactly as for normal polishing but avoid overloading the frontier of the sanded area. Sand lightly between coats.

How to clean french polish

Plenty of preparations are sold for this purpose, but not many of them are both effective and safe. The famous 'hodge podge'[1] beloved of antique dealers, has never been superseded. Merely

1. A mixture of beeswax and linseed oil, with a little turpentine.

rub on a little with a soft cloth and wipe carefully afterwards. The effect is usually excellent.

French polish to which a wax furniture polish has been applied: furniture which was originally french-polished has sometimes been treated with furniture polish at a later date. These useless accumulations can be removed with the aid of petrol (gasoline).

To renew 'tired' french polish: even if not actually scratched or flaking, french polish sometimes loses its brilliance after many years. A pad dipped in polish will quickly rejuvenate it.

Dismantling a cupboard

Are you moving to another house? If your family furniture includes grandmother's monumental cupboard or wardrobe – vast, heavy, the Immovable Mass, and you have made up your mind to take it to your new home, it can be taken to pieces; not a particularly hard job.

You will need help; the separate pieces, though not very heavy, will be awkward to handle. The first stage is to remove everything that comes apart easily, without special measures.

Usually, the cornice is a sliding fit, with nothing but gravity to hold it in place, and in most cases the top of the cupboard is fixed to it; so that removing the two together is just like taking off the lid of a box. In some cases, the doors are mounted on invisible pivots known to joiners and cabinet makers as pivot-hinges. These are small metal plates let into the top and bottom rails and fastened with screws. By taking out only the top *one* you can lift out the entire door.

Undo the two or three screws holding it and wobble the door to and fro to make the top plate slide in its groove. In reassembling the cupboard reverse the order, getting the plate into position first and putting the screws in afterwards, guided by the existing screw holes.

Hinges of the visible type present no problem. Open the doors at right angles and raise them so as to lift them off the pins.

Having got the doors off, take out the shelves. If they are a tight fit they can be loosened by a smart blow from underneath near one end, with the flat of the hand. Always take out a shelf by raising one end; the other can then be lifted from the cleat supporting it.

We now come to the tricky part of the job: *taking out the pegs*. Each main component of the cupboard is a complete entity: (1) the top, (2) the doors (already removed), (3) the sides and (4) the bottom. Never take the pegs out of these components themselves but only out of the pieces connecting them, namely (*a*) the top and bottom side rails, and (*b*) the rails of the back of the cupboard. Usually each bearer has two pegs, giving a total of eight pegs for the sides and from eight to sixteen pegs for the bottom.

You need a drift or a punch 10 or 15 cm long with a diameter slightly less than that of the pegs, say 5 or 6 mm. Joiners and cabinet makers frequently use a large nail with the point sawn off.

You will drive the pegs from *inside* to *outside*. Sometimes they protrude slightly on the inside. Tap them sharply to start them, taking care to hit straight. Then take a hammer and drift to get them out.

In practice, it is unusual for all the pegs to respond to the drift; some refuse to budge at all, others break up *in situ*. The only thing to do with these is to drill them out. You simply drill a hole exactly in the centre of the end of the peg, using a bit of exactly the same diameter as the peg; the peg turns into sawdust and its hole is left clean.

The conventional 8-mm twist bit, which is the right size for pegs, does not act well when used with end grain. If not accurately centred it leaves bits of the peg sticking to the sides of the hole. Use a plain gouge. This simple tool acts on a different principle from other types of bit, and centring occurs automatically through contact with the sides of the hole, thus leaving nothing behind. Not everyone is aware of the existence of gouge bits, which can be purchased from any well-stocked hardware store.[1]

After removing the pegs, take off the whole side of the cup-

1. If you prefer using an electric drill, don't try using a gouge bit. Begin by using a drill with a much smaller diameter and make a starting hole as a guide, about 5 mm deep; then drill out the peg with a drill of exactly the same diameter as the peg. Incidentally, make sure first that your electric drill has a big enough chuck; the smallest electric drills are not quite big enough for this job.

board, starting at the top. Use a wooden mallet, or failing that a hammer, and a piece of wood to prevent marking. Tap, or hit, all over the part being removed.

The first components to come away will be the top rails. It is a good thing to hold them in place while dismantling; if they are allowed to fall out the leverage may well result in snapping off a tenon inside its mortise. This precaution applies particularly to the top front rail; the rear ones are held in place by the panels. After removing the top rails, deal with the bottom ones in the same way.

Because the cupboard is about to lose one of its sides and will therefore be in danger of toppling over, prop it up from underneath with telephone directories, a small stool or any other suitable object. This is a vital precaution.

The back, which may be in two parts and constitutes the final operation, is unlikely to give trouble. A long or medium cold chisel will help you to lever it apart. Make marks with chalk or a pencil so you know which part corresponds to which; this is never a waste of time. Nothing is more annoying, when reassembling, than to find that the screw holes don't line up. And of course this always happens just at the end!

Reassembling consists of repeating the dismantling operations in reverse order. The old pegs, without exception, will have to be replaced with new ones. You can buy good oak pegs but they have one defect: they are four-sided; in other words, square in section, which would look rather crude on a fine piece of furniture. But don't make too much of a business of rectifying their shape; just take a flat chisel and smooth off their sharp edges to make them octagonal in section, which is quite good enough. After putting them in, cut them off flush with a panel saw or combination saw, smooth them (on the outside) with fine glasspaper, stain them to match, then wax them to seal the grain and give them the same patina as the rest of the cupboard.

A few hints

Suppose you have finished reassembling your cupboard and find that the doors don't close quite as they did before. Either they stick at top or bottom or have a tendency to swing open of their own accord. This is a matter of levelling. Experiment with thin blocks under the feet of the cupboard until you get the level right.

The doors and the cornice are the parts most likely to get knocked about in transport. Put the doors together with a blanket or a sheet of corrugated cardboard between them, and their inner sides facing outwards. Remember to take out the key and to remove any protruding metal fitments. Pad the cornice with corrugated cardboard and protect its corners with corrugated paper tied on with sisal string.

To reassemble a cupboard whose joints are a close fit and don't want to go together again, lay it on its side. You can then forcibly re-insert any tenons which are obstinately too tight. Rubbing with a lump of pure beeswax or paraffin wax will make it easier.

Gilt on wood

Gilding – whether on picture frames, carved panels, console tables, armchairs or pier-glasses – is interesting both for its intrinsic decorative value and for the distinction it adds to an *ensemble*. On the other hand, nothing is as vulgar as gilding carried to excess.

The keynote of gilding is preciosity, which characterizes the material itself, its handling and the preparations for its use. The application of gold leaf demands a skill most amateurs can never hope to acquire. It would be pointless to give the recipes and procedures used by the few remaining practitioners. There is nothing mysterious about the technique but manual skill is incommunicable and is not to be acquired from printed directions; it demands time, observation, practice and talent.

In gilding, 'less is more'

Fortunately, furniture or carvings, or an antique piece of any kind, or some motif forming part of it, can be re-gilded by others besides specialists. You can certainly undertake minor repairs and rescue operations, or enhance the brilliance or character of some small item picked up cheaply. We can help you here – *provided* you remember that repairing gilded pieces should never degenerate into a kind of outrageous face-lift. The age of a piece is part of its very essence and generates much of its charm. If, in the worn patches, the reddish foundation under the ancient gold leaf is glimmering hazily through, don't feel obliged to slosh the thing with gold all over and give it a brilliance which, so far from resembling the splendour of its youth, will be a meretricious parody. Always use gilt sparingly.

Gold leaf

People have always been looking for new tricks of the trade in order to bypass some of the operations involved, and, above all, for a satisfactory substitute for gold. We shall enumerate these in passing. But the worst difficulty of all, in our opinion, lies in building up the foundation (undercoat) before putting on the gold leaf. It is a matter of mixing parchment size or hide size with whiting (very fine plaster) – and Armenian bole (a kind of ochreous clay) and applying several coats of this mixture to the carvings or mouldings, using a very fine brush; each coat must be sanded and polished and the details re-carved. As can easily be imagined, the thickness builds up unevenly – in the hollows, for instance – and has to be corrected. As soon as a coat has been applied, the gilder taps the back of the piece to spread the mixture by vibration. After drying – which takes a number of hours – the whole business of re-carving, sanding and polishing has to be done again. The actual gilding, after such preliminaries, might seem to be a mere formality; but this is far from the case.

*

Do not attempt to renew the gilding on a picture frame, for example, unless the foundation is in good condition and the carving simple. Specialized firms can supply you with a ready-made preparation, a gilding base or sealer. Give the frame a careful cleaning, then apply this mixture with a very fine brush. It is absolutely essential to give it at least forty-eight hours to dry.

When the surface is well and truly dry, put on the actual gold. Gold leaf is sold in books, each leaf separated by a thin sheet of paper. The leaves are usually square 84×84 mm) and ·oo1 mm thick. The extreme delicacy accounts for the ease with which the material adjusts itself to the minutest details of a carving, and its readiness to adhere almost automatically to the foundation. A necessary precaution is to eliminate draughts in the room where you are working, otherwise your gold leaf will curl up into a useless, crumpled ball. Professional gilders use calfskin pads (with the flesh side outwards; in bookbinding and most other things it is the hair side which is outermost) made from the skin of a stillborn calf (which is peculiarly fine in texture), of perfect quality and protected by a thin frame. You can either procure one of these for yourself, or improvise a substitute. The fact that the gold leaf is supplied in books makes it easier to handle because each leaf is stuck to its protective sheet of paper and consequently holds more securely.

Carved and gilded frames
Apply the gold leaf, with no further preparation, straight on to the freshly applied 'mixture' and dab it gently with a cottonwool pad held between finger and thumb (the old craftsmen always used a hare's foot – possibly for luck!). Smooth the leaf down with little or no pressure; tap it with the fleshy part of a finger-tip if you like; a sable brush is useful for intricate details. Put on the gold leaves one after the other, with a slight overlap at the edges. Always do the smooth parts first, then those in relief.

Proceed gently: gold leaf is the easiest stuff in the world to fray or tear. If you have to shift a piece after putting it on, slip a piece of card under the edge or, better still, the tip of a gilding knife. If you need to use a small bit of leaf, say on a detail or a join, cut it with the knife and transfer it sticking to your finger-tip, which you can make sufficiently damp and greasy by first rubbing it on your forehead (this is what the professional invariably does).

Gilding looks far too new and uniform; it will need to be given a patina – 'browned', as the professionals say. Their recipe is to use fine agate, but you will be most unwise to imitate them. Protect your gold with a thin coat of varnish. Choose a varnish with a slightly brown tint; when the first coat is dry put on a second, concentrating particularly on the hollows so as to heighten the parts in relief.

Some useful expedients and variants

Genuine gold is expensive, but various copper alloys provide acceptable substitutes and are used on most 'gilded' mouldings sold commercially.

If you find the gold leaf not sticking down properly, try slightly dampening the surface of the mixture; but do this very cautiously and never moisten the area of more than one leaf at a time. Use distilled water.

To keep costs down, in the eighteenth century and for some time thereafter, silver leaf was used instead of gold leaf. The work was then given a coat of brown varnish, or of a preparation based on shellac, which made it look like gold. There were lots of workshop 'secrets' of this kind. Among the most interesting preparations is *vermeil*. The recipe is not easily translated into contemporary language, although all the ingredients can still be found in the highly specialized shops. *Rocou* (a red dye), 60 grammes; gutta percha, 60 grammes; vermillion, 30 grammes; dragon's blood (a resin used in making varnishes), 15 grammes; *cendres gravelées* (lees of wine, calcined), 60 grammes; the whole to be boiled with water until a syrupy consistency is attained. Directly before use, gum arabic water (120 grammes of gum to 0·93 litres of water) is added.

However antiquated this mixture may sound, it does give a fine warm glow to the 'gilt', even when the latter is silver! We have not quoted the procedure in such detail in order that amateurs should become fakers; far from it. But every time we have seen an example of this silver 'gilding' we have been struck by its genuine beauty; it has a character of its own, and we sincerely believe it has been restricted in use because of its reputation as a substitute, an 'imitation'; it is really a highly decorative material in its own right.

To end this rather specialized section, it is worth mentioning that gold leaf was often applied only to one half of an object – chandeliers and church ornaments in particular – the remainder being given a matching coat of ochre. This expedient was of course confined to pieces intended to be seen from one side only.

Gilding with paint

Take a brush . . .

How much easier it is to do it this way! You merely buy a pot of gold paint from a hardware shop and brush it on. But choose your gold paint with due care. And to make doubly sure, don't put it on straight away; do two or three trials on something else before setting about your delicate task. Different shades of gold paint are procurable; old gold, dark, pale, glossy, matt; choose the one best suited to the piece.

When the paint has dried, polish it with a little beeswax on a soft rag or piece of cottonwool.

Remember that for good results you will need at least two brushes, the smallest being for the carved parts.

When it has dried it looks too new and artificial, and different ways of giving it a patina leap to the mind. A brown varnish is the obvious answer. It always accumulates more in the valleys and less on the raised parts, giving rise to intriguing contrasts. You can also experiment with an ageing varnish or a cracking varnish (see the chapter on 'Pictures').

Varnish gilding

After thoroughly cleaning and drying a piece that requires gilding you can apply a special *vernis à colle d'or*; failing this, use an ordinary varnish, either clear or pale brown.

Use a small flat brush and avoid accumulations of varnish in the hollows. Then take a fat pinch of gold dust between forefinger and thumb and blow it at the varnished surface, to which the airborne gold will duly adhere. Only a little breath is needed, otherwise the gold will fly all over the place. Alternatively, you can use a paper tube or a squeezer-dispenser of the sort made for insecticides. Despite being rather unorthodox the method produces remarkably good results. When you have achieved an even covering of gold, leave your work to dry; when it has done so, give it a coat of melted paraffin wax with a soft brush. When the wax has cooled and hardened, polish it with a ball of cottonwool screwed up into a pad.

Removing gilt from a woodcarving
Stripping the gilt from a carved piece also entails removing the various undercoats.

To a bowl of very hot water add bicarbonate of soda and detergent powder (between 10 and 20 grammes per litre of water). The detergent is indispensable: among its properties is that of reducing the surface tension of liquids and hence of increasing their power of penetration.

Stir the solution well, dip a sponge into it and rub the old gilding. This will have to be repeated several times. The ideal method would be to immerse the object completely in the liquid, but of course this is hardly practicable.

Finish off by scrubbing with a stiff brush to remove the last particles of gilding from the crannies of the carving.

Looking after gilded wood

Cleaning gilded wood is almost no problem, because gold is not subject to corrosion and any dirt coming into contact with it is confined to the surface.

Good results are obtained with soapy water, applied with a small brush to penetrate the details of mouldings and carvings. Ordinary alcohol (such as methylated spirits) is also an excellent agent, perhaps the best, for the care of gilt; it should be followed by polishing with a chamois leather.

One can also use one of the workshop recipes of the professional gilder. After brushing all the dust out of the surfaces, add a few drops of bleach to the white of an egg and beat until thoroughly mixed. Apply the mixture with a flat brush; the resulting film, when dry, can be picked off like scales, taking any dirt with it. In another version of the recipe, a handful of salt is used instead of the bleach.

At all times, avoid any cleaning process which might get out of hand once the original undercoat is laid bare. This – the layer of whiting and parchment size – needs nothing stronger than water to dissolve it.

There are a few popular recipes which are amusing to try and, as we know from personal experience, safe.

Onion juice, or grated onion, can be put on with a brush and will brighten but not damage the gold, which should then be washed with water and polished with a soft cloth or chamois leather. If the gilt is very dirty a satisfactory result can be obtained by rubbing it with a sponge dipped in undilute vinegar, and then washing it with water.

10 Grandfather clocks

Grandfather clocks

A short course in horology for the lover of antiques

Clocks worked by weights have existed since the early Middle Ages. Examples have been preserved whose parts are made of forged iron, and whose design is very similar to that of the revolving spit. The pull exerted by a weight on a cable wound round an axle caused the axle to rotate. A gear-train at once made this rotation smoother and translated it into a slower speed. The earliest clocks had *one* hand only. The time, or an approximation to it, was read from the position of the hand on a graduated dial: the space between each number and the next was divided into halves and quarters; sometimes these divisions were indicated on a smaller, concentric dial.

This arrangement was accepted until the sixteenth century, when another hand was added to divide the hour into minutes and in some cases into seconds; and a third had made its appearance, indicating the days of the month; and a striking mechanism with a bell was incorporated.

It was the nineteenth century which brought the grandfather clock, in its wooden case, to the apogee of its development.

But, as we have indicated, it had clearly existed for centuries before that period.

If it is a French clock and has straight sides (without bulges) and is narrow, made of thick wood, carved and designed to contain a comparatively small mechanism, it was probably made before the last century. It often exhibits the stylistic attributes of its period: panels with symmetrical divisions, each in the form of a curled, pointed arch, denote the age of Louis XIV; panels with asymmetrical divisions (but balancing each other symmetrically), with carved floral decorations – Louis XV; plain rectangular panels, surrounded by carved rustic decoration, 'pearl' borders and grooves – Louis XVI.

The straightness of the sides is of course related to the mechanism they enclose: the pendulum was only relatively important. Often the bob was just a very small lump of lead. In slightly more sophisticated designs it took the form of a sun or a face (in the reign of Louis XIV); sometimes it was a disc of polished brass; but it was only a few centimetres in diameter (4, or at the most 5).

The 'belly' which was soon evolved, giving the case a likeness to that of a double-bass, was called into being to accommodate the considerable increase in the diameter of the bob. Confining ourselves to the cabinet-making side before dragging the reader with us into the mysteries of the works, we note that the case was in step with *regional* stylistic development and was thus always in complete harmony with provincial furniture. Later there was a tendency towards uniformity: cases were made of lightweight woods such as pine or poplar and painted in several colours or 'grained', and ornamented with rustic décors, little flowers, flower sprays and similar attributes. This was the terminus of development.

Although, as we have said, the shape of the case varied with the style of the period, the chief factor determining it was the size of the mechanism and the pendulum. The latter is a valuable pointer to the age of any clock. Any pendulum consisting of a simple bar, flat or round in section, ending in a small weight (sometimes with a figurative design) or disc, indicates a period prior to the nineteenth century.

In that century, the polished brass disc developed rapidly; its surface was enlarged; originally resembling a small lens made of metal, it reached the size of a saucer and finally of a plate. An indication of age, but not one which denotes the period at all exactly, is the method of adjusting the pendulum: the earliest method was undoubtedly that of sliding the bob up or down on the rod. The decadence of the long-case or grandfather clock is marked by the appearance of the ornamented, coloured and animated bob. Clocks with this feature hardly go back farther than 1900. They represent a boy stealing apples and a farmer's wife chasing him with a broom, or even a donkey nodding its head at a carrot; sometimes a little girl on a swing.

The type of pendulum in French clocks has further secrets to impart. The suspension of the bob from the mechanism has a hidden language of its own. Putting it simply, two types occur most frequently, those in which the bob hangs on a string or rod respectively. The first is thought to be the older.

Turning aside, for a moment, to English long-case clocks, we find that they are less varied in shape and style. They come in different sizes but the shape is normally straight up and down, two square cases, one for the movement and one to allow a balanced base, sandwiching the narrow rectangular pendulum case between. Developments in movements went step by step with similar developments abroad. As to decoration of the case, English clocks tended to be elegant rather than showy, and naturally, in the eighteenth and early nineteenth centuries, the case reflected the styles of Chippendale, Adam, Sheraton and Hepplewhite, to match them with the fashion of the time.

Let us leave the pendulum and consider the face, which is often what most attracts the eyes and interest of the amateur. In the oldest clocks the dial is of brass or pewter; sometimes the numbers are painted with enamel on raised studs fixed to the dial. Later, we find dials enamelled all over, ceramic dials and, on some country clocks, wooden dials. Here again, local and period styles make themselves felt in the general character of the dial, its quality, and the character of the numbers. The latter may exemplify an ancient clockmaking tradition, a 'IIII' consisting of four upright strokes instead of the more logical Roman IV.

The surround of the face is another illuminating feature. If it is of heavy, moulded metal, with decoration embodying a cock or pierced arabesques for its pediment, you may be looking at a pre-nineteenth century antique clock. A surround of smooth wood or iron sometimes indicates the Georgian period. After that, one finds brass backgrounds with highly luxuriant repoussé decoration, almost always rustic in character. When this decoration is polychromed it is a sign the ultimate incarnation of the long-case clock has been reached.

Let us now go into greater technical detail – remember we are concerned solely with the long-case or grandfather clock.

Let us look at the escapement. This indispensable component consists of a toothed wheel revolving step-fashion in time with the pendulum, and a rocker called the pallets (see sketch). When the axis of the escape-wheel is vertical, the movement is older than when it is horizontal.

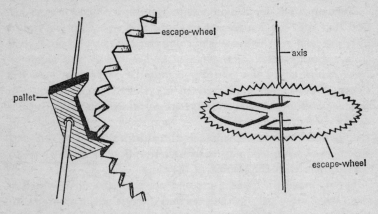

At each swing of the pendulum, one pallet goes up and the other goes down, releasing one tooth of the escape-wheel in the process. This ingenious device is not present in all old clocks. In some, there is a 'verge escapement': a metal rod with a pallet at each end (see the sketch). This is obviously the ancestor of the first

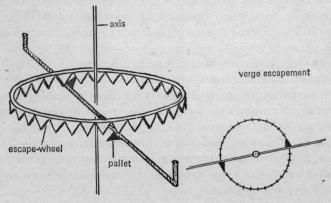

mechanism described. However, these indications are only a general guide. It is a well-known fact that rural clockmaking did not always march in step with technical improvements elsewhere. Examples are known of reasonably accurate clocks made entirely of wood. These rudimentary movements really did work and probably still do, provided that woodworm hasn't ruined them. The same cannot be said of the wooden watch displayed in Magdeburg museum, whose face, pinions, hands and case are all of wood. The only exception is the driving wheel, which is of bone. The craftsmanship is astonishing but the contraption plainly doesn't go.

How to put a clock into position

The advice given here is concerned only with enabling your clock to work properly.

You have set up the case as nearly plumb-true as you can, hooked on the weights and wound them up. *Remember that the big weight is hung from the escapement and the small one from the striking mechanism.* That is, when the weights are of different sizes, which they usually are. In this as in many other things, exceptions are common: the weights may be equal.

Your sense of rhythm is about to be put to the test. You are going to put your clock 'in beat'. This is done *by ear*: listen carefully to the sound of your clock. The ideal is to have the same time-lapse between *tick* and *tock* as between *tock* and *tick*. Correcting an uneven rhythm may require a little trial and error but will not take long. What you have to do is to level not the case but the mechanism. Provide yourself with some small pieces of cardboard and bristol, open the case, lift one corner of the mechanism, slip a sufficient number of pieces under it, and listen. Always put thin pieces first, replacing them with thick ones if necessary.

Check for accuracy – you will soon find out if your clock is gaining or losing. The error is easy to correct by altering the length of the pendulum. Raise the bob if the clock is losing, and vice versa. You will easily discover how to do this. Usually there is a small screw *below* the bob; sometimes the bob is so arranged as to stay in place by friction alone.

Cleaning a clock

Dust and cobwebs accumulate when a clock is neglected over a long period. You will have seen that the mechanism is reassuringly robust, so don't worry about using vigorous methods.

If you can, relieve your clock of its hands, dial and the cords for the weights, dust it with a flat brush which you can dip in paraffin (kerosene) if you like, then put it in a boiling solution of washing soda (50 grammes to the litre). You will get excellent results by adding ammonia (one or two tablespoonsful) to the water, and potassium oxalate crystals (half a tablespoonful). Try to bring the water right up to the boil, because its ebullition then takes it into the smallest details of the works. Rinsing and drying are essential. Give it a good long rinse in running hot water and dry it with whatever means are available: a hair-drier, or in front of an open oven or on top of a radiator, etc.

Don't on any account lubricate the pinions, it would be the surest way of attracting dust and having to repeat the cleaning after a short while. Just use a little vaseline on the bearings, without excess or mess.

A clock cleaned like this can go on for years without giving trouble, provided it is lubricated every couple of years. To complete the job, take some fine emery paper and remove any rust from the metal case which houses the movement. And a coat of anti-corrosion paint on this case will do no harm.

The cords should be changed if necessary. The hempen cords used by the old clockmakers can be advantageously replaced by woven nylon cords; these are easy to get from yacht chandlers.

When putting on new cords, take care to see that the turns lie *evenly*, *touching one another*, on the roller; they will then automatically return to the right position whenever they are wound up. Making them the right length is easy: the weights should just touch the bottom of the case (or in some instances the floor) when the cords are unrolled.

11 Ivory

Ivory

Ivory has been familiar to man from the days when mammoths walked the earth and has been worked by man ever since some very remote period. The Venuses of the Aurignacian period – figurines characterized by voluminous femininity – are a two-fold conundrum for specialists, because of the sculptural skill shown and also because it is hard to say just when these works were made.

It is also highly probable that ivory as an artistic medium was known from remote antiquity in China. However, it is not until a later period that tangible evidence appears of a more highly developed art, at once directed to more practical ends and endowed with more purely decorative qualities. In 1930, a dig carried out under two French archaeologists, MM. Schaeffer and Chenet, in the ruins of Ras Shamra in eastern Syria, opposite Cyprus, produced some very fine vases carved in ivory, which are thought to date from about 1400 B.C. Two years later, in 1932, excavations begun by an Anglo-American expedition and continued in 1934 by the Welcome Archaeological Research Expedition, at Tel Duweir, an ancient site in Palestine, 50 km south of Jerusalem, brought to light numerous objects carved in ivory, notably a scent bottle in the likeness of a woman in a long tunic, and a portrait-miniature.

Many similar finds in Egypt make it plain that ivory-working was widespread under the Pharaohs. This noble material was used not only as a medium for ornament in temples and palaces but for making chairs and other articles of furniture, some of which have been recovered from Egyptian tombs.

The Phoenicians, traders, provided the Greeks with ivory and taught them the art of carving it.

Homer, in the *Odyssey*, makes it clear that his compatriots used ivory for ornamenting bridles, keys, chairs and beds. They also turned it into scabbards and combs.

Homer, again, has handed down the earliest recorded name of a craftsman in ivory, one Ismalios. By fixing small sheets of ivory, skilfully fitted together, to a wooden frame, Phidias made large statues, some as much as 10 or 12 metres high! Among them was the famous Zeus of Olympia, regarded as one of the 'seven wonders of the world'.

Rome used ivory for statues of deities, sacrificial appurtenances and the interior decoration of temples. Senators were officially entitled to an ivory sceptre and seat, at their own expense. The tradition has acquired a niche in literature: Flaubert, in *Salammbô*, lyrically lists sumptuous doors, magnificent beds, thrones and household furniture, all of ivory and gold. Victor Hugo, in *Les Tables tournantes de Jersey*, treats us to an imaginative description of Carthage: '... It was a giant city. It was sixty leagues in circumference and possessed six thousand temples, three thousand of which were of marble, two thousand of porphyry, six hundred of alabaster, three hundred of jasper, fifty of stucco, forty-five of ivory,' and so on.

Byzantium, in becoming the capital of the Eastern Empire, also became the heir of Greco-Latin art. Intense activity in ivory working was one of the results, attested by priceless icons on ivory sheets.

Much later, towards the eleventh century, ivory carvers devoted their energies to the production of things for everyday use. It was at this period that France began outstripping the other European countries, so that by the thirteenth century it can be said that *ivory was essentially a French art*; it had become an industrial art in the modern sense of the term.

In the centuries following this development, the raw material gradually became more plentiful as a result of the great voyages and the new geographical discoveries achieved through them.

The Low Countries and Germany, strengthening their ties with the great traditions of Western art, manifested a certain brilliance during this period. The makers of small objects in ivory and kindred materials were not mainly concerned with fine art; most of their work went into a multitude of practical things, such as knife handles, snuffboxes, fans, shuttles, croziers, the heads of walking-sticks, rosaries, flasks, etc. Under Louis XIV, the billiard table made its appearance in the *salon*; the balls and the cues were of ivory. At the same period the clavichord and the spinet became hugely fashionable; in both, ivory inlays were common, and of course the keys were covered with ivory.

During the reign of Louis XV some very beautiful toilet sets appeared; the most celebrated were those of the Marquise de Pompadour and the Comtesse du Barry. Importation of the raw material turned Dieppe, one of the ports for the Near East and Africa, into a centre of an industry which rapidly attained prosperity.

There is a tradition that ivory was being carved at Dieppe as early as the fifteenth century. Villaut de Bellefond, whose book *La Relation des côtes d'Afrique appelées 'Guinée'* appeared in 1669, wrote that two ships equipped and manned from Dieppe brought back so much ivory that the citizens began carving it themselves. However, this account notwithstanding, it has to be said that no evidence exists that the craft was practised on any considerable scale at Dieppe at such an early date. In Rouen, on the other hand, ivory carvers are included in the list of artists named by the guild statutes of the 'imagers' (painters and sculptors) as early as 1507.

It was probably a hundred years later when a certain number of craftsmen in ivory set up shop in Dieppe. In 1694 the English author and diarist, John Evelyn, published a work in which he observed that the town was full of all sorts of curiosities fashioned in ivory. By that time the craftsmen of Dieppe had become pastmasters in ivory working. The delicacy of its carvings and other products was spoken of everywhere as being far in advance of anything that other towns could boast.

Much later, the Revolution was to deal a fearful blow to Dieppe's ivory industry, whose customers were mainly English tourists and a few other travellers. By 1794 there were only eight merchants, two ivory workers and six carvers.

During the First Empire the craft gradually picked up again; the fall of Napoleon caused a temporary crisis, but after that the output and sales of ivory articles in Dieppe completely regained their former prosperity.

Today, only Dieppe Museum bears witness to the fame and prosperity which ivory and the ivory craftsmen once conferred on the town.

Real or imitation ivory

The dictionary informs us that ivory is a substance of a milky colour and of the same character, chemically speaking, as bone, but denser and more homogeneous in texture.

It occurs in the form of tusks: those of the elephant, rhinoceros and walrus, and the teeth of the hippopotamus.

However, the ivory most generally used, and the only one with a legal right to the name, is that produced by the elephant.

This falls into two classes: hard and soft.

Hard ivory is yielded by elephants whose lives have been spent in wooded, shady surroundings, in the proximity of rivers, streams and marshes, in the humid climate of Guinea, Gabon and the Congo.

It is heavier than soft ivory and has no grain, that is to say no vein-like markings. In colour it is a fine, roseate white which turns whiter still with age. It is used by sculptors, including sculptors of figurines; miniature painters, toymakers and similar craftsmen; and cutlers.

Soft ivory comes from open country with a dry climate. The animal's tusks gradually lose their 'sap' through continued exposure to hot sunshine. As a rule their points have splintered. Soft ivory hails only from certain parts of Ethiopia, Egypt and the coast of Zanzibar.

Being tender and highly resilient, soft ivory is particularly sought after by the manufacturers of billiard balls and piano keys, because it enables uniform results to be achieved.

The African elephant is the species which provides practically all the ivory used by sculptors and craftsmen in both Europe and Asia.

The geography of ivory

The following are the principal ivory producing regions of Africa and the characteristics of the ivory they yield:

Senegal (now Mali Republic) : grey ivory, semi-soft, of inferior quality.
Sudan (now Mali Republic) : grey ivory, semi-soft and soft.
Guinea: hard ivory of the best quality.
Ivory Coast: grey ivory, soft and semi-soft, deficient in quality.
Niger: hard and soft ivory.
Cameroon, Gabon, Angola: hard ivory, pink in colour.
Zaire: green ivory, both hard and soft.
Cape: pink ivory.
Mozambique: grey ivory, hard and soft.
Tanzania, Kenya: hard and soft.

Africa's biggest supplier is Zaire. Zaire ivory comes from the eastern part of the state, mostly from the districts of Stanleyville, the Bas-Véla and the Ituri.

Before the Second World War, the big ivory sales took place every three months. The most important were those held in Antwerp, London and Liverpool, in that order.

Today, these sales are virtually non-existent.

In fact, since 1920, when 300–400 tons of raw ivory were exported annually, the tonnage of ivory exported from Africa has fallen by over two-thirds. Legal restrictions on hunting, not demand, have diminished the amounts of ivory sold year by year. A review of the amounts sold, in relation to the respective countries contributing to the total, shows that the effects of legislation have differed from one African country to another. Some of these countries had already almost disappeared from the world markets as early as 1940; particularly the French possessions, in which killing an elephant was a legal offence.

The weight of a tusk varies according to length and diameter; a weight of 75–80 kilos, with a length of 2·3–2·5 metres, is by no means rare. The price of raw ivory is stable: 40–80 francs per kilo, according to quality. Imports of ivory into England are at a similar low level, with prices varying with quality between £5 and £10 per 453 grammes. Scarcity has forced the English dealer to comb the country's junk markets for old ivory. From the middle of the eighteenth century right through to the end of the Victorian era, ivory flowed into the country in ever increasing quantities, both by way of trade and in the form of trophies or souvenirs. Ivory was one of the fruits of an expanding empire, and by the time of Queen Victoria's Golden Jubilee, there can have been few 'respectable' homes in England which could not boast a brass gong supported by two decorated ivory tusks.

Legal protection for the buyer of ivory

The advent of plastics dealt ivory a mortal blow, not only in the manufacture of useful accessories but also in the field of pure art. It also encouraged fraud. Fakes, in both Eastern and Western styles, made entirely of plastic, have appeared in the market. Ivory has a much higher density than plastic; comparison between the weights of a genuine object and a fake shows up the difference. To mask it, some fakers have adroitly used ivory dust (an easily recoverable workshop by-product) as a filler to mix with synthetic resins, the resulting conglomerate being uncomfortably close in appearance to the real thing.

One large chemical firm has even succeeded in reproducing the grain and veining possessed by certain qualities of ivory.

In this case, and sometimes in the preceding one, the substance is sold honestly under the name '*ivoirine*' or '*ivorine*'.

An English industrialist, however, blithely attaches the name 'ivory parisiana' to a substance of his own composition! Fortunately, such 'innovators' are blocked by a decree of the French Ministry of Agriculture dated 17 October 1950, which lays down standards governing the sale of objects made of ivory.

Article 2 stipulates that the word '*ivoire*' shall apply only to the natural substance of which elephants' tusks are composed.

Article 5 forbids the sale under the name '*ivoire*', with or without any qualifying terms, of any substance containing a quantity, however small, of anything other than ivory.

Article 7 requires that when any of the products or objects covered by the decree are visibly labelled '*ivoire*' in a display or shop, accompanied by objects made of an imitation material, the latter must be clearly labelled with the name of the material or with the word 'imitation'.

Article 8 forbids the use, in any form, of any indication or mode of presentation, such as a drawing, illustration, sign or symbol of any kind, or of any verbal appellation capable of creating, even phonetically, any confusion in the mind of the purchaser concerning the nature, origin, characteristics or composition of the products or objects by the decree.

In addition to ivory, the decree covers tortoise shell, amber and meerschaum.

The decree is of the first importance for the customer's protection, being deliberately framed so as to preclude equivocal or alternative interpretations. The protection provided in France by the government decree is paralleled by the Trades Description Act in Britain.

Repairing ivory

Ivory is worked in the same ways as wood. It resembles wood in possessing a grain but is much more flexible, so that it hardly ever snaps under the craftsman's hand. Time and atmospheric factors, especially excessive dryness, make ivory deteriorate and give it a tendency to split; a knock or other clumsy move may then cause a break.

Fortunately, a break in a piece of ivory is nearly always clean, almost geometrically so. The two parts can be stuck with the same adhesives as for wood. It is noticeable, however, that the adhesive does not always bond well; it should therefore be reinforced mechanically by the use of pegs, miniature dowels or the like. This requires extreme care. What is the best way of going about it?

On any projecting member, such as the arm of a statuette or a comparable part of an ornament, try putting in a metal pin (of copper or brass). But it must not show through in the light; thin ivory is translucent, almost transparent. If the thickness is insufficient you will have to make a delicate little dowel from a piece of scrap ivory. In either case, dowel or pin, you will have to bore a hole, taking care not to let it go right through from side to side; you want the repair to be invisible once the adhesive has set. Ivory is very easy to drill; the drill must run rather slowly.

Ivory responds to vinyl adhesives and is not stained by them. Moderate cramping is desirable. Ingenuity and the shape of the object will determine whether you use adhesive tape, elastic bands or suchlike.

A modern method: when dealing with a fragile object use an epoxy adhesive alone, without pinning. Don't leave any dribbles of adhesive, clean them off with spirit, and allow the adhesive to harden in a warm atmosphere: 20 °C if possible, and in any case not lower than 15° or 16°. The repair will be permanent and invisible.

A heavier piece, with a broken projecting portion, can be treated in the same way but with a slight variation. Drill a hole in each surface of the break, as if to house a pin uniting the two pieces; fill both holes with epoxy resin and reinforce it with a few fibres taken from a bit of glass fibre cloth. The other end of the fibres, of course, goes into the other hole. You'll find it quite easy to lay the fibres together compactly so that they make a little pin, as it were, and do not catch on the sides of either hole. Cover the rest of the surfaces of the break with a thin film of adhesive. Put the two parts together and cramp them. Allow about twenty-four hours for hardening, in a warm place.

Additional hints

A few fibres are enough; don't feel you must cram the hole with them. A characteristic of epoxy resins, which makes them so important, is that after drying they are of almost mineral hardness; if spread in a thin layer they are indestructible, but if used thickly they may snap off clean, like glass; hence the necessity of reinforcement.

Warped ivory

Ivory sometimes warps if exposed to humidity over a long period, or if the object is a thin one such as a comb or hairbrush.

Before the shape can be corrected the ivory must be softened. Place the object in water to which about one fifth of nitric acid has been added, and leave it to soak for three or four days. This makes it fairly translucent and surprisingly pliable. Bend into the required shape and leave it to dry. It will soon regain its normal stiffness and opacity. But avoid putting it for any length of time into hot water; this would soften it.

An advantage of this method is the help it gives in marquetry, or in covering an object with an overlay of ivory. An important point is to remember that, whenever you are sticking thin slips of ivory on a dark surface (wood or metal, as may be the case), a sheet of white paper should be stuck on first as a backing, otherwise the support will show through the ivory.

The patina of ivory

Specialists will tell you that ivory is white, and that a patina can be obtained only by some dubious external application. Various ivories age in different ways, depending on quality. Most kinds do not turn yellow with age, in fact they get whiter.

For those who simply must have a patina here are a few safe recipes.

Expose the ivory to woodsmoke (but not to heat). A slight tarry deposit will settle in the recesses and after drying for a few hours will form a sturdy, durable patina. Rub it with a woollen duster.

Decoctions of tea and chicory also yield a brown or golden patina. Simply paint the liquid on, and leave it to dry.

'Natural' wood stains, such as walnut or Cassel extract, give excellent results. With time, they may even sink in to some depth.

Some exotic brownish-red ivories are tinted by the natives with betel nut or areca nut.

The Chinese are pastmasters at tinting ivory and use a wide variety of colours, blue, green, red and so on. Nowadays they use either ordinary chemical colouring agents, or dyes which are much the same as textile dyes.

To those for whom oddities hold a special appeal we present two recipes, the first of which gives ivory a bronze-green shade.

Put into some nitric acid as much bronze as it is capable of dissolving, then place the ivory in it overnight. The result is a very beautiful green. (But we must add that this is a dangerous thing to do with a valuable ivory piece.)

A truly Far Eastern method of giving ivory a golden yellow patina is to carry it next the skin. Bulky articles are not recommended!

How to look after ivory

Household recipes for cleaning ivory are plentiful and mostly quite harmless, especially those using lemon juice.

Just use soap and water.

Ivory can be polished by coating it with Spanish whiting mixed with lukewarm water. As soon as the whiting has dried, rub with a chamois leather.

Brushes, combs, dressing-cases, knife handles and piano keys can be kept in condition by regular cleaning with a mixture of Spanish whiting and methylated spirit.

When an elaborately carved ivory piece has become encrusted with dust or tenacious dirt, give it a bath for a few hours in fresh milk (not boiled or pasteurized). Then brush it with a stiff brush and rub it with a soft cloth until it is perfectly dry.

To whiten ivory

To give ivory a milky, matt appearance coat it with turpentine and let it stand in the sun for a few hours.

Hydrogen peroxide 120 volumes (see page 6) is a safe means of making ivory white. The effect is immediate. You can either dip the ivory in the liquid or paint the liquid on. In the latter case, use a piece of cottonwool; a brush would be damaged. Rinse and dry.

There is an old recipe for whitening and cleaning ivory which is still applicable provided certain precautions are observed. Dissolve some rock alum in water, place the ivory in it, bring the solution to the boil and keep it on the boil for an hour. If any dirt still remains, brush it off. Wrap the ivory in several thicknesses of wet cloth and let the whole thing dry in the air.

The purpose of the wet wrapping is to slow down the drying process and avoid the little cracks which develop when ivory passes too abruptly from one state of humidity to another.

Preserving ivory

Ivory always remains a living substance, and if kept in too dry an atmosphere it cracks and rapidly deteriorates. Equip radiators with humidifiers, and never expose ivory pieces to excessive warmth (such as that from a light-bulb); they will then remain in good condition for many years.

*

One of the most original collections of ivory we have seen is undoubtedly that of M. R. Brejoux, the President of the Chambre Syndicale de l'Ivoire. Every item in it was made by M. Brejoux himself. He produces replicas of old ships on a scale of 1/100; a unique achievement, without a parallel anywhere. M. Brejoux has invented a technique for producing ivory 'thread'; from a single 'vein' of elephant's tusk he can make threads of 0·3 mm diameter for the rigging of his ships, the simplest of which has cost him 3500 hours of work!

His vocation sprang originally from a curious incident which deserves a place in 'mini-history', anecdotal history. In 1964, preparations were under way in France to receive President Kennedy on an official visit. To André Malraux, Minister of Cultural Affairs, occurred the idea of commissioning the crafts-men of the Musée de la Marine to make a model of the *Flore*, the first ship in the fleet of Louis XVI to salute an American vessel; a *de facto* recognition by France of the United States, at that time not yet officially constituted. A very suitable present to offer John Kennedy, as a former naval officer; but though the idea was excellent in itself the Minister felt the gift was hardly adequate for a visiting Head of State. To match the result with the intention Malraux decided to have the *Flore* modelled in ivory, and the commission was handed to M. Brejoux – who was faced by un-foreseen technical problems because everything, including sails and ropes, had to be made of ivory, unassisted by any other material.

The finished model, a wonderful achievement, was thrust into limbo by President Kennedy's death. The foundation item in M. Brejoux's collection was thus a doubly historical reject. But, so far from being disappointed, he had discovered his life's passion. The *Flore* was followed by a model of the *Astrolabe*, the ship of the great French navigator Dumont d'Urville. Next came four *chebecs* like those ordered by Colbert from shipyards in the south of France (a *chebec* or *sciabecco* is a Mediterranean three-masted vessel, lateen-rigged). These were highly elegant but terribly difficult, the pieces being so tiny: thirty-two blunderbusses, twenty-four cannon, and sails of a special design – the latter alone kept M. Brejoux occupied for eleven months.

In May 1960 he finished a slave-ship, the *Ouragan*, and, using some very rare research information, began re-creating the *Paradis*, the ship that bore St Louis to the Holy Land.

A collection of this kind is not only invaluable in its own right; it is a testament of professional devotion and skill.

Before closing this section, I must draw attention to the fact that the Victoria and Albert Museum in London has one of the finest collections in the world of fine ivories of every period.

12 Marble

Marble

Certain disasters, such as a commode with a shattered top, or a mutilated mantelpiece can be mended almost invisibly.

Follow our advice: it will serve you well in these days when marble masons are scarce, marble expensive and bills high.

A smooth, straight break, like a cut, is always a disadvantage. Its very regularity makes it hard to camouflage. Moreover it may slip during cramping.

Let's examine the commonest case: an irregular break – which in many instances has already been mended years ago.

1. With a file, a wire brush or coarse emery paper, clean up the surfaces of the break and carefully remove all traces of old glue.

2. Prepare your adhesive. We recommend a two-part epoxy resin adhesive. Nothing else, as yet, makes such a strong joint. The stuff comes in two tubes, the resin and the hardener. Mix the requisite quantity with great care.

3. Coat both surfaces. No blobs anywhere; use a small, flexible spatula; aim at producing a fine, even film of adhesive.

4. Bring the pieces together, having planned in advance how you are going to keep them there; with carpenter's cramps, elastic bands (cut from an old inner tube), pieces of wood and so on. A marble slab in a piece of furniture is unlikely to present any snags. A mantelpiece, and some other things, may not be so easy. On small objects, elastic bands come in handy in various ways as does sticky tape. More detailed advice is really not possible; special cases abound and solutions vary infinitely.

When using your file or emery paper, collect the resulting marble dust in a dustpan or the like. If necessary you can supply yourself with extra marble dust – marble flour, as it is called – by gently scraping the back or underside of the marble. Mixed with a little adhesive this powdered marble makes a mortar for building up a small chip or smoothing the edges of the fracture. For white marble, talc gives good results.

Having glued the pieces together with absolute accuracy, take care to remove any dribbles of adhesive with alcohol and a bit of cottonwool.

Twenty-four hours later, when drying is complete, polish your work. Buy the finest flower paper obtainable and use it wet. By polishing the glue-line you will find you can make it practically invisible.

Sometimes, however careful you are, you won't be able to find all the fragments from the break. After gluing, splinters of considerable size will be missing. Don't worry. At a paint-shop you will find a range of assorted shellacs which can be poured hot into the cavities (always remember that shellac should be melted with a hot iron; never use a flame, which would char it). Having filled the hole, polish as above.

Modern technique to the rescue

Two-part adhesives, which attain mineral hardness, provide an extraordinarily strong joint. They are a remarkable advance on earlier methods. However, other two-part preparations have recently been developed which actually imitate marble. Their adhesive power is lower than that of the epoxy resins, but for building up a missing chip, even quite a large one, they are truly sensational.

When buying, match the shade carefully.

When using, mix up no more than you can use quickly, because with some makes the setting time is rather short. Follow the manufacturer's instructions about adding the hardener, and mix thoroughly.

Watch out for one thing: the mixture must be forced well down into the interstices; use a spatula, and press hard. The consistency, which is that of thick honey, makes this easy, but you must avoid letting bubbles form; subsequent polishing will turn them into holes.

Hardening occurs without delay. After a few minutes the adhesive becomes resistant to finger-pressure and gives off a strong smell. Make use of this intermediate period, while hardening is incomplete, to remove dribbles and to smooth your work with a wood chisel, a rasp or a file. When the work is completely hard you can still shape it a bit, but with much greater difficulty. The plastic can then be polished with flower paper, as above.

We emphasize the advantages of this method. No cramping; simply bring the parts together and hold them in place by hand for the short time required for polymerization; and carry out the finishing process at once – no tedious wait for setting.

Learn to make a mould

In order to reconstitute a missing corner or a moulding, or a motif on a mantlepiece, say, or a clock, you will have to take a mould from an intact portion. There are two methods, both very simple. *Plaster of Paris* is the first: the better, but if anything the trickier, of the two. The part to be reproduced must be coated, in moderation, with oil (use vaseline, or salad oil on a rag). Fix up a 'fence', a miniature shuttering, of cardboard, to prevent the plaster from running. Plaster, unlike cement, is used pure, and is mixed not by adding water to it but by adding it to water (use about the same quantity of water as you require of wet plaster).

As soon as the plaster has 'worked' and has become a pourable slurry, pour it into the shuttering, meanwhile tapping the shuttering with a small tool of some sort so as to vibrate the plaster and cause it to enter the details.

After a few minutes the plaster will be hard. Take the mould off; you will find the motif imprinted in reverse. All you have to do is to place the mould opposite the part to be reconstituted, and insert the plastic.

But watch it! Some motifs have undercuts. Check carefully before committing yourself; make sure the mould, once made, can be removed.

Modelling paste (e.g. plasticine): the ideal method if the motif is a simple one. You take an impression by pressing the plasticine on to the motif.

But take care not to distort your improvised mould while taking it off. Speed and simplicity are the advantages of this method. The disadvantage is the danger of distortion. This can be avoided by supporting the mould with bits of wood or cardboard.

The latest way: for coping with complicated motifs, which would be very tricky to mould by either of the above methods, latex elastomers offer endless possibilities.

These elastomers consist of latex in a paste or liquid form; they vulcanize at ordinary atmospheric temperature and humidity. Their viscosity enables them to penetrate the smallest cranny. After vulcanization, the mould, which remains rubbery and flexible, is easily withdrawn without damage, and is unaffected by the plastic used for building up the missing part.

Care of marble

Marble is cleaned with soft soap (rinse well afterwards). Failing this, a very weak solution of washing soda is quite suitable.

Virgin wax is the best protection for marble. The wax can be diluted with a drop of paraffin (kerosene).

How to remove spots and stains

Marble absorbs stains: they often mark it in depth. The most dangerous enemies of marble tops are wine (the foot of a glass or the bottom of a bottle) and vinegar and lemon juice (because they are acid).

Repolishing is the treatment for affected marble. This is a job for the professional, though one can get a fairly good result oneself with flower paper.

Ink stains are not necessarily permanent. Hydrogen peroxide (see page 6) may surprise you by removing the stain completely. If only partially successful, repeat. The hydrogen peroxide must have a chance of operating in depth if the ink has sunk some way into the marble, which is porous by nature. If necessary, add a few drops of ammonia to the hydrogen peroxide.

Rust often causes deep stains on white marble. Iron oxide penetrates insidiously and becomes very difficult to dislodge. Try hydrogen peroxide first. If this doesn't work, buy a little sodium bisulphite; only a few drops will be needed. Dust the stain with zinc filings and pour on the bisulphite. Wait for a few minutes; then wash the mixture off with water. If the result is still a failure there is another remedy: the rust removers used by laundrymen.

But be careful, these substances usually have an oxalic acid base and may attack the marble slightly. Do a trial; dust the stain with rust-remover, wet it with a dropper, wait for five or six minutes and rinse. If the marble has become rough at the spot treated, go no further; if it hasn't, try again, allowing more time for the treatment to work. Roughness, if only slight, can easily be rectified by polishing with flower paper.

How to recognize antique marble

There are several signs by which antique marble can be recognized:

General appearance. Its finely polished surfaces shows signs of wear in places.

By placing a rule on it, you find the surface is *not perfectly flat* (the old marble masons didn't use machines).

The underneath, or the part against the wall, is roughly cut (examine it in a slanting light).

Grooves, mouldings and decorative carving are slightly irregular (handwork again).

An interesting check: Whenever you have to remove a slab of marble for repair, you have a chance of examining the piece of furniture it covers. Usually, cabinet makers signed their work, but in concealed places. Commodes were generally signed *under the marble,* on the rails of the top drawer.

Your best procedure is to place a sheet of paper over the marks you find (they are often indistinct); rub with pencil lead or a graphite block; the signature, if such the marks really are, will then show up clearly.

13 Paintings

Cleaning paintings

Once more we must warn the reader that the cleaning of paintings of any value should be left to the expert. You can become an expert in using the methods described below, but this takes long practice. Old pictures get so obscured with the passage of time, and their richest harmonies and brightest colours so muted, that their decorative value is much reduced. To restore a work of art to its original character is a mark of respect towards both the art and the artist.

The worst enemies of paintings are changes of temperature, variations in the humidity of the atmosphere (a ban on all central heating!), and the assorted smoke with which the air of our cities is saturated (and which frequently deposits a film of greasy or acid matter). Flies, too, have left their tenacious traces on many an aged canvas. Finally, the protective varnishes with which too many pictures are laden have cracked, and sometimes become almost opaque. In many cases, 'contemporary taste' has demanded the use of a coloured varnish, which has darkened with age. You may want to try and clean your own pictures and obtain their original form.

This will involve delicate problems in which, technical questions apart, your own intuition and instinctive touch will be your surest guide.

Taking the picture out of its frame
Don't pull out the nails which hold the picture in the frame. Simply bend them upwards, and straighten them again when you put the picture back.

Minor cleaning – anyone can do this

This may sound amateur or like an old wives' tale, but is perfectly valid. Cut an onion in half and rub the picture with it. From time to time shave a thin slice off the onion so that you are always working with a clean surface. The combined chemical and mechanical effect of the juice and stratification of the onion will do the trick and make no stains on the painting.

Let us now pass to other, progressively more difficult, methods.

1. *Lukewarm water, ordinary household soap* (*not toilet soap*) *and a soft sponge* are a safe combination; they cannot possibly harm the picture. The sponge should be only just damp, so as not to soak the canvas unnecessarily. Use the soap sparingly and rinse thoroughly as you go along. The method is undeniably effective and the success is easy to gauge, were it only by the colour of the water which comes out of the sponge after rinsing!

2. *Washing soda* is used by the greatest experts; both the strength of the solution and its application demand great care. Dissolve a pinch of soda in a cup or saucer filled with lukewarm water; stir well, to make sure all the crystals are dissolved. Take a piece of cottonwool, dip it in the solution and wet one corner of the canvas by way of trial. After a few seconds you will gain an idea of the strength of the solution. If there is little or no effect, add another pinch of soda to the water, stirring as before. Holding the cottonwool delicately between thumb and forefinger, rub lightly with a circular movement. Rinse copiously with another piece of cottonwool dipped in pure water. Don't underdo the rinsing, otherwise the soda may leave white marks after drying. By following these directions you will achieve a cleaning-in-depth which will not damage the paint in any way; it will recover its vitality to a surprising degree.

*

Note: This method is particularly recommended for ancient icons, which have usually been exposed to candle smoke and rough handling.

We must emphasize the limit beyond which an amateur should never venture. Do *not*, without long experience, attempt to remove varnish with soda. Indeed, only a varnish which had been applied comparatively recently would respond at all. We advise a different method, at once highly effective and easier to control.

Removing varnish with alcohol

Set yourself up with all the requisites for completely removing the varnish, namely:

> a bottle of ordinary *spirit* (alcohol), a bottle of *turpentine*, two large pads of *cottonwool* or, better, *cellulose wool* (which does not catch on the paint and leave threads behind it). Also have some dry cottonwool within reach.

The principle: De-varnishing, as you will have suspected, is at once delicate and easy (the speed of the operation is one of the risks). So, before explaining the method, a word about the principle.

Alcohol first softens the varnish, then dilutes it; turpentine, on the other hand, instantly inhibits both these reactions.

It is therefore appropriate to have a turpentine pad ready in one hand while de-varnishing with an alcohol pad in the other – because alcohol dilutes paint and its effect *must* be arrested in time.

However, turpentine also exerts a desiccating action on paint and this is specially harmful to old pictures, which have already become very dry in the course of years. Some restorers always counteract the effect by mixing linseed oil with the turpentine. This is an excellent precaution which you should follow too. Another which deserves mention consists of 'feeding' an old picture with linseed oil before any cleaning or de-varnishing operation. For this purpose use the linseed oil which is sold expressly for artists; it is refined and will penetrate all the better. Coat the whole surface of the picture with it fairly generously, using a sable brush; lay the picture flat if possible (to avoid runs), protected against dust, and leave it for twenty-four or forty-eight hours.

You can then set about removing the varnish, confident that you have insured against risk as far as may be.

Removing varnish: the job itself

Begin in a corner. With your alcohol pad, rub with a circular motion. In the first few seconds, nothing will happen; then the pad will check very slightly, as if sticking and the varnish will disappear. Keep the pad well wetted with alcohol so that it does not catch on the surface. You will see the picture becoming lighter and brighter with every pass you make. Don't be too severe; arrest the reaction with turpentine; if you find you have arrested it too soon you can start again with a clean pad, the alcohol will produce its effect as before. Carry on until, by gradually shifting from place to place, you have done the whole canvas. Do not try to treat the whole surface at once, you would not be able to keep a proper check on your work. When stripping large areas, such as skies or fields, step back from time to time to gauge the effect in relation to the rest and to make sure you are not over-doing it.

When you think the varnish has been adequately stripped, swab thoroughly with turpentine and make sure that no part of the surface is still tacky.

Don't hesitate to impregnate the whole canvas with turps and linseed oil. Besides completely preventing further action by the alcohol, it will give new life to the paint and the fibres of the canvas or to the wood.

Re-varnishing

After drying (which will take a few hours at most) comes re-varnishing.

This is essential both for preservation and for appearance. Choose a matt or a gloss varnish, whichever you prefer, but make sure it is a clear one (we are against brown varnishes, they darken a picture unnecessarily). Every good art shop sells varnishes put up in small bottles. Use a flat brush, starting at the top of the canvas with varnish criss-cross motion. Work in a good light, so as to avoid thin patches or runs. Don't load your brush too heavily, and leave the picture to dry in a dust free place.

A general check

When dry, the picture can be re-framed. Take this chance to check that all is well with the cord, pins, rings, etc.; a worthwhile precaution.

If the canvas is slack (which it may be, though cleaning will help), it must be stretched taut. The stretcher (the wooden rectangle on which the canvas is braced) usually has small wooden wedges at its corners. A few careful taps with a hammer on these will restore tension.

But some stretchers have no wedges. In such cases the canvas will have to be re-attached to the stretcher with upholstery tacks (use the smallest size) and drawn tight with the aid of small pliers with flat jaws.

You will be surprised by the transformation that simple cleaning can effect.

A few extra hints
Before starting to clean a picture in depth, try to fix its values in your mind's eye. ('Values', pictorially speaking, are the relations of intensity between the colours.) This will be your guide in keeping your work uniform. The values, after cleaning, should be the same, but brighter.

Modern pigments and varnishes are much more sensitive to alcohol than those of past centuries. Watch out for this and be doubly careful.

Cracking is a valuable pointer to the age of a picture. Short cracks, forming rectangles: earlier than the eighteenth century. Irregular cracks: eighteenth and early nineteenth centuries. Concentric circles: nineteenth century. These simple, over-schematic distinctions form the foundation for a more expert appraisal.

Transferring a painting to a new canvas

In a picture, the support is usually more vulnerable than the paint. Unfortunately, their fates are interdependent. Works of art of high quality demand the attentions of a specialist. We cannot sufficiently repeat that, without a regular apprenticeship, it is out of the question for you to attempt re-canvassing a picture, let alone to transfer the paint itself to a new canvas.

But there is nothing to stop you trying your hand on a torn canvas which is almost past praying for, some daub disinterred in an attic or picked up at a junk shop.

After this initial experience of re-backing a picture, followed by a few more, you can start thinking of rejuvenating that tired lot you inherited some time ago from a relation; pictures you might have thrown away if their aura of family associations had not stayed your hand.

We shall try to convey in real terms the principles both of re-backing and of transferring; but please don't cast us in the role of sorcerer's apprentice.

Let us start with the simpler of the two: *re-backing*.

This consists of sticking a new piece of canvas on the back of an old one which is deteriorating or worn.

Before embarking on this operation, which requires care and delicacy, clean the picture (as described in the previous chapter); also get the back completely clean, so that its accumulated dust is not trapped by the glue, or paste rather, which you will be using.

Take your picture and expose it to steam. This has a very definite purpose: the excessive dryness of old canvas or paint may otherwise absorb too much of the water contained in the flour paste, and unsightly 'efflorescences' might result.

Very carefully detach the canvas from the stretcher and lay it on a smooth, flat surface, painted side uppermost. Give the paint a coat of flour paste. Take some very thin paper (tissue paper is ideal), stick it on the paint, apply several more coats of paste and add more paper. The thicker the protection the safer the picture will be; accidents can always happen. Don't hesitate to put on additional layers of ordinary paper, even newspaper.

This stage being completed, the next is to stick on a piece of new canvas slightly larger than the old one. First give a plentiful coat of fish glue to one side of the new piece, taking care to spread the glue evenly. Do the same to the back of the picture, then bring the two into contact and press them firmly together to make sure they stick all over. Take a warm iron and iron the new piece, pressing hard; this will make the glue still more liquid and help it to penetrate the smallest interstices of both canvases, until they become as one.

Let the reinforced picture dry thoroughly, then nail it to its stretcher, making sure of the tension as you do so. Proceed to remove the layers of paper from the paint surface with a sponge dipped in a solution of bicarbonate of soda in lukewarm water.

The layers will gradually loosen and become easy to take off. The paint itself will need to be well washed with water.

Before reinstating the picture in its frame you can give it a coat of much-diluted paint of the same colour as the dominant colour of the composition, all round the edges of the fabric, for better preservation.

To transfer or not?

This is an extreme case. A picture may be in an even worse state, with its canvas so worn and frail that the paint is beginning to come off in little flakes. In some cases the canvas is actually crumbling into dust and is quite incapable of acting as a connection between the paint and a new piece of canvas; so the paint must be transferred.

This operation is definitely more delicate than re-backing; the task of removing the paint entire from the old canvas and transposing it to a new one demands relentless concentration.

If the paint is tending to flake off, begin by sticking to it a piece of gauze, slightly oversize. This will hold the paint together throughout the operation and will also act as a reinforcement to the layers of tissue paper which are to be stuck on for protection in the way already described. Wait until all this is quite dry before very carefully removing the canvas from the stretcher. Remember that it is fragile and must be handled tenderly.

So much for Stage One. We now embark on Stage Two.

Put the canvas, face downwards, on a flat surface. The job now confronting you is to get rid of the old canvas. If it is extremely thin and tenuous, use very fine glasspaper; if stronger, a coarser grade of glasspaper. Some specialists prefer pumice stone. The aim is gradually to wear the canvas away until you reach the back of the paint. Concentrate very carefully when the abrasive comes into contact with the paint. Thoroughly wipe off the dust you have made, then stick the painting on to new canvas with a vinyl acrylic adhesive.

Every restorer has his own secret method for the sticking. Some of them manage to obtain natural adhesion by applying a hot iron to the back of the new canvas after laying it over the paint. But this, we feel, is not an example to emulate. Another method is to use fish glue, as in re-backing. In this case it is essential to give both the underside of the painting and the new canvas a thin coat of formaline before putting on the glue. The reason is that adhesives of organic origin (glues made from bones, hides, casein, fish, etc.) are always open to attack by moulds and micro-organisms. Formaline prevents these infections, which would destroy the adhesive film. The advantage of fish glue is its great flexibility. Other glues render the canvas excessively hard and rigid, eventually producing cracks which affect the preservation of the paint.

One of the 'secrets' known to restorers is the use of zinc white or white lead to join the paint and canvas together (white lead contains carbonate of lead, which is highly toxic; it must therefore be handled with care). This is supposed to give the paint a support having affinities with its own composition; which is true. But as white lead and zinc white are generally supplied in the form of a stiff paste, the usual practice is to dilute them with linseed oil. A fact not universally known is that linseed oil has a deleterious effect on the flax from whose fibres painters' canvases are woven (*linseed*, and the flax which is the raw material of *linen*, are closely related, botanically speaking). So that using linseed oil is 'one step forward, two steps back', and is bound to cause deterioration of the new canvas within a more or less foreseeable future.

Our own experience leads us to prefer a vinyl acrylic adhesive. A moderately thin coat should be given to the paint and to the new canvas. Avoid, at all costs, laying it on too thick. The adhesive must never soak through the canvas and exude from the surface.

After a few day's drying, the paper can be removed from the picture surface as described in the preceding section.

A painting on wood is also capable of being transferred but this is a task usually left to specialists; and even they are often unwilling to undertake an operation fraught with so many difficulties.

The process was discovered by Picault and Hacquin, two picture-restorers of the mid-eighteenth century.

It consists of applying a protective shield of paper in the usual way, and then of making shallow saw-cuts in the back of the wood, generally in the form of small squares which can be removed with the help of a chisel. With further help from a rasp or a small plane the thickness of the wood is further diminished; from time to time it is wetted with a sponge to make it swell, so that it comes away more easily; and so the underside of the paint is eventually reached. It need hardly be stressed what a delicate technique this is.

There is, however, one peculiarity which makes the task easier. To prepare a wooden panel for painting it was usual to lay on a fairly thick ground, and this in most cases has proved to be less permanent than the paint.

This ground serves as a 'frontier' to your work; moreover it is bad at holding the fibres of the wood, which therefore come away nicely.

Can you hang a picture?

Hanging a picture securely is often a nightmare for the amateur. Solid walls, cavity walls; soft, friable partition or impenetrable cement – every case is a law unto itself. Add to this the decorative problems involved, and the whole thing begins to look hopeless. However, without in any way limiting the imaginative possibilities, we can perhaps put forward ideas from which everyone can select those which satisfy his own tastes and requirements.

Some principles of decoration

Hanging a picture demands thought. Whether it be a painting, engraving, reproduction or photograph, its position will be determined by its character, shape and size (and weight). Let us look at a few examples.

Over furniture: the width of the picture should never be greater than that of the piece of furniture above which it is hung. Beware of frames which are too massive or otherwise obtrusive, overwhelming their surroundings. A picture so framed should be frankly isolated in the middle of a bare wall. If the piece of furniture is heavy or massive, the picture which bears it company should be of opposite format (if the piece of furniture is wide the picture should be tall, and vice versa; horizontal contrasting with vertical); and the picture should be hung fairly high.

A tall, narrow picture: this shape is not often used in painting; it is commoner in looking-glasses. The obvious place for it is between two windows or doors, or in an entrance hall or other small room.

A collection of pictures: many pictures, close together, are a combination to avoid unless the pictures are of fairly high artistic merit. A line of pictures side by side (or one above the other) is permissible in a passage. In any much-used room, hanging should be carefully planned not to disrupt the general harmony. You should determine an imaginary line to act as a basis; hanging should be such that the bottom edges of the frames, large and small alike, rigorously follow this line. But avoid symmetry. Two small pictures accompanying a large one should form a triad: the bottom of one of them should be level with that of the large picture; the top of the other, level with the top of the large one.

Height: it is always inadvisable to place pictures too high. They should be at eye level. This applies particularly to small pictures. If for some reason you do decide to hang a picture high up, tilt it forwards accordingly.

Frames: a serious problem! When choosing a frame for an old picture the style of the latter must be respected; but the character of the subject will assist you. A florid Louise Quinze frame, all volutes and arabesques, would be out of keeping with the ordered severity of an architectural prospect or a middle class interior by a Flemish painter, but would be in perfect harmony with a battle scene or a *fête galante*, swarming with figures.

Contemporary works are the hardest

Hardly any general rules can be laid down; however, here are a few guide-lines. The frame should carry an echo of the dominant colour in the picture. For example, the paintings of Utrillo, so many of which are views in Montmartre – creamy white walls, the pure white of the Sacré-Coeur, and skies consisting of blue-white or grey-white clouds – demand light frames, shimmering like ivory, to suit the harmonies of the composition.

Very modern works can be classed with prints, in which the important thing is the structure or graphic quality of the subject; this should monopolize the attention; hence a frame is not always necessary. A very slim frame, of the natural colour of the wood, or painted black, gold or some very delicate shade, will be almost unnoticeable but will put a boundary between the picture and the space surrounding it.

Practical hints

'*X*' *picturehangers* have certain advantages, confirmed by long experience. Their steel pins penetrate well in most materials and do little harm to walls. The range of sizes from No 0 to No 4 is adequate to deal with most situations; it allows for light, normal, heavy (two pins) and very heavy objects (three pins). Note, however, that concrete may make the pins buckle or break. It is important to know how to avoid this by driving them in correctly. Accurate little taps, *in line with the pin*, are the answer.

'*Swedish*' *hooks* in moulded plastic are a new addition to the decorator's armoury; somewhat surprisingly, their three pins are very short (about 5 mm). But it must be admitted that they hold very well in extra-hard wall materials such as concrete, mortar, brick and stone. In plaster they are not always so satisfactory and the manufacturers therefore supply an extra steel pin, 25 mm long, which goes in deep and reinforces·the effect of the three little ones.

Expansion bolts: for hollow walls and soft materials, the manufacturers of expansion bolts have developed extra-strong hooks from which heavy weights can safely be suspended.

Mirror-hooks are essential for supporting decorative objects of great weight, such as engravings, whose weight is substantially increased by the glass (large engravings are often held between two sheets of glass, to keep them perfectly flat).

Forged mirror-hooks, which have to be bonded in, do not concern us: we always prefer the screw-in type. They work very simply: a sleeve is pushed into a hole drilled in the wall, and into this is screwed a metal component embodying a head with a groove to accommodate the mirror. The head is supplied drilled and tapped to receive a decorative cap which hides the screw.

To hang a very heavy engraving, three mirror-hooks can be put in at the bottom to support it, and another at the mid-point of the top edge to prevent it from tilting forward. Great care is

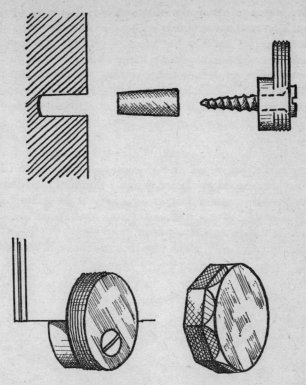

necessary to ensure that the weight is taken up evenly by all three hooks, not just one or two. This is achieved by drawing a line on the wall, level with the lower edge of the engraving, and drilling the holes exactly on the line. Don't screw the hooks right home; put the engraving in first, then screw tight.

Hints on special cases

Concealing hooks: in all cases when the picture cord has to come up above the top edge of the picture to ensure that it hangs straight, the hook, of necessity, is visible. It can be concealed by adding a decorative motif in bronze in the form of a circular flower, a fleur-de-lis or a star; it is also possible to buy ready-made decorative hooks. An unframed print can be held in place by a little bronze hand, for example.

Clips: glazed prints or reproductions are often hung by means of clips. This goes marvellously with modern works and is also an excellent way of holding the sheet of glass at the back. The difficulty lies in fixing the picture to the wall. The usual method is to have a piece of steel wire connecting the hooks. But this is unsatisfactory; the tension on the wire tends to pull the hooks towards each other and in any case the attachment to the wall is visible. There is a very neat way out of the difficulty; it only requires a little care and accuracy. Right-angle cup-hooks are screwed into the wall and their heads left pointing horizontally instead of vertically, all in the same direction. Make sure of inserting them in the wall exactly in the positions where the clips will come. All you then have to do is to hold the picture up and slide it sideways, so that the head of each hook enters the tubular channel in the corresponding clip.

When buying hooks, make sure they are the right size to fit the clips.

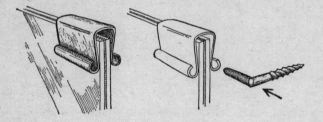

14 Pottery and porcelain

Pottery and porcelain

Earthenware, faïence and porcelain, rightly regarded as being some of the most fragile materials, pose mostly simple problems to the amateur restorer.

Modern epoxy resin adhesives are better for sticking broken pottery or porcelain than all older types of glue, and make the rivets which china menders used to use unnecessary.

Nevertheless, technical progress often clashes with professional tradition and only gradually replaces methods which did give satisfaction. One of the arguments most frequently put forward by professional restorers is the hardness of epoxy resins, a characteristic which (I quote) 'makes any subsequent restoration very difficult'. Can they really mean this seriously? If a restoration has been properly carried out, surely it will never need doing again? Anyway, from our own considerable experience with these resins, if an object already repaired in this way breaks for a second time the new break will not be in the same place.

Another advantage of epoxy resins, which nobody will dispute, is that an object so repaired 'rings' as it would have done had it never been broken. As many people know, there is a test which shows whether pottery or porcelain has been repaired or has a hairline crack somewhere, a hidden weakness: you balance the piece on three fingers and, with the other hand, tap the rim smartly with a finger nail. If the piece has no defect it gives a good, clean ring. A plate broken into several pieces will, after being repaired with an epoxy resin, ring like a new plate.

*

Epoxy resins are sold in two parts – usually two tubes – the resin so-called and the hardener (see chapter on 'Adhesives'). To ensure adhesion and hardening repairs should be carried out in a temperature of 15 °C or more. You can even heat them to make them act faster (up to 22 °C during polymerization, and up to 146 °C once hardening has occurred).

After carefully mixing the two components in accordance with the manufacturer's directions, put a thin, very even coat of adhesive on each surface to be glued. If any traces of glue are present from an earlier repair, scrape them off with great care. The success of the whole operation depends on thorough preparation. The delicate question in repairing ceramics is how to hold

the pieces together. Solve this problem before sticking them. Use rubber bands and/or medical sticking plaster. There is a reason for preferring the medical variety: it is the only kind which is perforated to allow air to pass, and it is slightly elastic. When you have stuck it on one of the pieces to be held together you can stretch it before sticking it to the other piece, producing a tension which helps to cramp them together. Clothes pegs, cramps, weights and so on, may all be useful.

An important warning: if the shape of an article broken in several places is such that you have to repair it by stages instead of all at once, never leave any overflows of adhesive on a part you are going to stick later. If an overflow is left to harden you will be in trouble when you come to stick the next piece.

Another essential warning: there is NO satisfactory way of removing dribbles of epoxy resin once they have hardened. So it is vital to remove them while the adhesive is still soft, with a wad of cotton-wool dipped in alcohol. Leave the repaired work under pressure, without handling it at all, for about twelve hours.

A considerable advance in repairing ceramics is the recent development of a one-part epoxy resin which is a contact adhesive. The two faces of a break, coated thinly with this adhesive, should be accurately brought together; adhesion is immediate and final, ingenious cramping arrangements become unnecessary, and multiple breaks can be mended without delays.

Old techniques

Here are a few well-tried and effective recipes which in the past – even the recent past – have been the basis of sound repairs.

Foremost of all we may place the remarkable '*mastic La Victoire*', a low grade form of dental cement, which has been the salvation of generations of repairers. Sold in powder form, it is mixed with water to the consistency of thick honey, and is left to stand for a few minutes before use as an adhesive. Its resistance to heat and water is very satisfactory. A chip or small hole can be effectively repaired by building up with *mastic La Victoire*.

Fish glue, mixed in equal quantities with acetic glue (which is not easy to find), undoubtedly holds well but is vulnerable to humidity. Moreover both surfaces must first be moistened with formalin (a 40 per cent solution of the gas formaldehyde), a disinfectant preventing attack by micro-organisms, which are often partial to fish glue.

If you like picturesque recipes here are two which, despite sounding home-spun, are still used. *White of egg*, well mixed with finely ground sieved lime, makes a mortar which sets fairly rapidly and is effective even on delicate porcelain.

Gruyère cheese, macerated in water for three days, is mixed with two or three snails (without their shells); the resulting paste (admittedly rather revolting) is then mixed with an equal quantity of quicklime, well pounded and free from lumps. This strange preparation will enable you to repair not only ceramics but, apparently, glass.

A variant of the same recipe (whose efficacy we are not in a position to judge): curdled milk, two or three *red* snails (slugs?) and quicklime.

The temptation to find a rational explanation for everything leads us to compare this formula with the well-known principle of casein glues (curdled milk) fixed with an alkali (lime). But the role of the slugs and snails must also be accounted for. Possibly the idea was to make use of the slime secreted by these creatures, which is certainly sticky. Or perhaps we should push the reasoning further. Casein glues are sensitive to micro-organisms, like any other alimentary product. Industrially, they are stabilized by the addition of antiseptics. This might be the role played by the snail; which, as we know, has a place in the pharmacopoeia of popular medicine, notably in the treatment of infectious conditions of the respiratory tract.

Contemplate traditional recipes with an open mind. This is desirable for several reasons. Observation plays a large part in repairs to furniture and other antiques. Every material has a life of its own: some are *alive* – wood, ivory, bone and some textile fibres; others are *capricious*, such as metals, whose oxidation develops in accordance with the unpredictable interplay of atmospheric factors; *none is inert*, appearances notwithstanding: they are susceptible to heat, cold, light and humidity.

Finally, awareness of ancient solutions helps in making an intelligent choice of new products and sometimes gives us a better appreciation of their advantages.

Building up a missing fragment

Sticking broken parts together again, however effective, obviously works only when all the parts are there. Building up a chip or other small fragment which is missing can be done, but it is useless attempting it without adequate knowledge of the materials described below.

Barbotine

This is very white, very finely powdered clay which regains its plasticity on being mixed with water. 'Barbola' is very similar.

Ceramic cold pastes

These composite materials, developed for use in schools, are easy to model, and set by exposure to the air, acquiring the hardness of ceramics. The resources of this new material for the restorer are immense. But they are not always fluid enough to make a satisfactory join with the object to be completed.

Plastic resins (coloured, quick-setting)

These should not be confused with epoxy resins, whose role is adhesive. Though comparable in nature with epoxy resins they differ in appearance and even more so in adhesive strength. They too require a hardener.

Sold in the form of a fairly thick paste, in different colours, the range is small but sufficiently varied for most ordinary repairs. Since they are frequently used for restoring marble you may find them classified as types of marble such as Carrara, Siena, etc. As you will colour them yourself this does not much matter, except (obviously) that you will not choose a dark shade to reproduce a pale one.

These resins are often our salvation; they are quick setting and, after curing, acquire almost mineral hardness. They demand considerable deftness, as they cannot be modelled. Their consistency, something like thick honey, has both advantages and drawbacks. For filling in a missing chip in a flat place they are unrivalled, especially as there is no perceptible shrinkage during polymerization. The wall of a vase or cup, or the edge of a plate, can be easily mended by making a plaster mould of an intact part which has the same shape, and slipping this mould over the broken place. The resin is then put in (from the inside if the object is a vase or a cup, which is first laid on its side). For a small hole, a piece of card or sticky tape takes the place of a mould. If you have no plaster, children's modelling paste is ideal, especially since an exactly accurate mould is unnecessary, as you will find for yourself; imperfections are very easy to put right.

Polymerization takes place fairly rapidly, so use the resin

immediately you have added the hardener. As soon as the chemical action gets under way the stuff goes tacky, and this is when bubbles may give trouble; when you polish the repair you may find an air-bubble or two, which will form holes. You will have to fill them in or else do the whole job again. For a few minutes the resin, though already fairly hard, will be of a consistency that can be worked with a flat chisel, a gouge or a razor blade. This makes it very easy to restore a moulding (e.g. at the edge of a plate or dish). But watch out: polymerization is going forward steadily, so do the rough finishing quickly, with edged tools; after that, you can carry on with a carpenter's rasp, followed by a file, the only tool which will make any impression on the resin once it has hardened. Final polishing will be effected with paper.

One can, at a pinch, use the same resin both for sticking and for rebuilding; the great advantage is that no cramping is needed, setting being fast enough for the pieces to be held in place by hand until perfect adhesion has occurred. In our opinion, these resins are not quite fluid enough to avoid leaving an excessively thick film along the line of the break.

For a small chip on the rim of a dish, plate or vase, *barbotine* offers a very satisfactory means of repair, and is easy to paint or enamel afterwards.

Cold ceramic pastes make it possible to completely reconstitute a handle, a spout or a foot; your ability will determine the success of the repair. Follow the manufacturer's directions carefully; especially as the composition of these pastes varies. Some behave rather like plastic resins. There are also special 'cold' glazes for these pastes, usually sold at the same shop; artists' colourmen, chiefly.

'Adhesives for pottery and porcelain' is a general title under which various products are sold; some are just conventional glues, others are epoxy resins. It may be difficult to tell which is which, even though the brand name is a reassuring one; in that case hold fast to the definitions given here. If you ask for an epoxy resin you will of necessity be given a branded product, but there will be no confusion.

'*Enamel*' *adhesives:* these are sold for repairing chipped enamel.

Generally used for kitchenware and the like, they are very white. As it is impossible to alter their colour, they can hardly be recommended for repairing pottery. And their whiteness is too harsh and glaring for porcelain.

The potentialities of 'cold' enamel

A beautifully executed repair should be finished to the same standard. 'Cold' enamels (obtainable from firms specializing in artists' materials and equipment) are supplied in an excellent range of colours, making it possible to match either the ground-colour of a plate or its coloured motifs. Try out the required shades a few times before colouring the actual object. We know from our own experience that 'cold' enamel tends to be perceptibly more brilliant than the 'hot' (i.e. fired) enamels on pottery. Don't give up; let the new enamel dry completely and then reduce its brightness with wet-and-dry or a little pumice powder. Cracks can be imitated with a very fine watercolour brush, taking care to match them to those of the original.

If you fight shy of cold enamel, and especially if you have a complicated, many-coloured design to restore, gouache will be found completely satisfactory. When dry, it can be protected with a coat of clear varnish.

How to look after pottery and porcelain

This is absolutely straightforward. To wash them just like ordinary dishes, with a suitable detergent, is the best way; rinse carefully in very hot water, and dry with a good, absorbent tea towel. Then rub them with methylated spirit on a bit of cottonwool or rag. When the spirit has dried, polish them well.

For porcelain with raised or gilded decoration, use very little detergent, and no scourer.

Terracotta responds admirably to hot water and a few soda crystals. A stiff paintbrush will get into the details. Rinse in clean lukewarm water and leave to dry.

15 Silver

Silver

In ancient Egypt, as early as 3500 B.C., silver was rated considerably superior to gold as a precious metal: its value was twice that of its weight in fine gold. Although there appear never to have been any silver mines in Egypt, a certain amount of silver was extracted from Nubian gold, which had a silver content of between 9·7 and 24 per cent. This process was very imperfect, and one of the so-called silver war trumpets found in Tutankhamen's tomb can be classified as 'white gold'. i.e. gold with a high proportion of silver in it.

Early in the third millennium, silver from the mines of Anatolia probably supplanted the gold obtained from mines farther to the east. Archaeological sites at Ur and Susa have yielded a few examples of goldsmith's work; however, silver, unlike gold, suffers heavily from oxidation and the results of excavation are modified accordingly.

In Europe, silver was known as a precious metal in 2000 B.C. Deposits were scarce and metallurgists were compelled to extract silver from lead, which in the raw state always contains varying amounts of silver. Six centuries before Christ, the Greeks minted the earliest known silver currency.

The mining, smelting and working of silver on a large scale, however, may have originated on the coast of Peru about 500 B.C., or on the high plateaux of Colombia. The conjecture is forced on us by the fact that the metal was not much esteemed under the pre-Colombian civilizations; possibly because they had not mastered the technique of extracting it. Only in the thirteenth century of our own epoch, under the Incas, do we find a large number of useful, precious or ornamental objects made of a silver and copper alloy. The world's main silver-bearing deposits are in

Central and South America. The *conquistadores*, having failed to find Eldorado but succeeding in pillaging the natives' gold, had thereafter to make do with silver, which they dispatched in large ingots in their famous galleons. This made it so plentiful that it was used for common everyday objects, at least by the well-to-do. Previously, gold had held pride of place on rich men's tables. The inventory of Charles V's possessions, in his will, lists seven dozen large gold dishes, followed by one hundred and thirty-eight silver dishes, evidently regarded as small fry by comparison.

After the time of Charles V the Spaniards caused silver to become commonplace all over Europe. Silverware, in the modern sense, dates from then.

Nevertheless, there were powerful Western countries – England and France in particular – which for the preceding two centuries had tried to protect the standard of silver by strict control. In the thirteenth century, in both countries, there emerged guilds or *jurandes* whose hallmarks were accepted as official standards by all. Later, silver became coin of the realm; and authority, whether royal, imperial or republican, jealously protected itself against counterfeiters. Since Charles V's time, every government has laid down standards for the various grades of silver and has kept production under surveillance. In England, though standards of gold and silver had been jealously protected by guilds already well established in the twelfth century, no royal charter gave them sanction until Edward III granted the first Goldsmiths' Charter in 1327, the first year of his reign. This charter was only confirmed, after a solemn petition, by Henry IV in 1404, and again by Edward IV in 1462. It would seem that the English monarchs were content to allow the guilds to conduct their own affairs without interference and, on the face of it, it seems extraordinary that they resisted the temptation to impose taxes on manufactured articles. But we must remember that the guilds were part-time bankers and many a loan reached the exchequer at the royal request. It was left to Pitt the Younger, in 1784, to exploit this source of revenue by imposing a duty of sixpence per ounce on all plate manufactured for sale. This led to the introduction of a punch mark of the King's head, by way of receipt, struck at the time of assay. This tax at varying rates has never since been relinquished, though the King's head punch was abandoned in 1890.

Like the French, English seventeenth-century silver is extremely rare. Both Louis XIV and Charles I were great melters of plate, which went to help their armies in the field. The Puritans under Cromwell were no better.

One thing for which the English must be eternally grateful to the '*Roi Soleil*' was his revocation, in 1685, of the Edict of Nantes which had protected the Huguenots from persecution since 1598. This led to a wholesale exodus of gold- and silversmiths and craftsmen of all kinds to Holland, England and the settlements in America. It was these Huguenot artists in silver, with names such as Courtauld and de Lamerie, who were responsible for the pre-eminence of English silver throughout the eighteenth century.

Until the end of the sixteenth century, only three punch marks were commonly found on English plate – that of the maker, who used a symbol registered at the guild as being exclusively his, the mark of origin (for Edinburgh a castle, for London a crowned leopard's head, and for Dublin a crowned harp), and the assay mark to denote sterling quality. Early in the eighteenth century, the maker's symbol was replaced by the maker's initials.

The study of silver marks has been extensive, and those who wish to go into the subject further should consult the authors listed in the footnote below.[1]

This continuous official participation in commercial transactions involving silver makes it at once simple and more complicated to identify antique silverware and the metal of which it is made. The regulations (for instance, the position of the hallmark is laid down according to the type of article), *plus* the fact that we possess complete records of almost all the hallmarks, marks and countermarks which have obtained since the regulations began, make it possible to date and place the origin of any piece, and the

---

[1] Tardy, *Les Poinçons de garantie internationaux pour l'argent*, 'Annuaires d'horlogerie-bijouterie', 18 rue des Volontaires, Paris. (*Poinçon* means hallmark). This covers the whole field, including, of course, French and English marks.

Bradbury's Book of Hallmarks, J. W. Northend Ltd, West Street, Sheffield, S1 3SH. This is an invaluable pocket guide and condensed *vade mecum* for the collector of English silver.

standard of the silver. On the other hand, the huge number and variations of these marks, their meanings, their countries of origin (every country has its own), compel both the serious amateur and the professional to refer to specialist works in which all the hall-marks and regulations are classified.

How to recognize silver

Officialdom's guarantee is expressed by the hallmarks indicating the standard, that is to say the pure silver content, of the piece. However, pieces sometimes crop up which have somehow eluded official control. Moreover, when visiting a junk shop or an antique dealer you may find that superficial examination or the absence of information leaves you dubious about the metal itself, especially with a piece that is dirty or oxidized.

In a case like this you can hardly resort to tests based on chemical reactions, unless you make a practice of carrying the necessary kit with you!

Experienced dealers have two very simple methods on which they rely. The first consists of testing by hand; feeling the weight of the article. Silver, like any other metal, has a specific gravity. Experts claim to be able to recognize silver simply by appreciating its weight in the hand. They may be right; but how does one acquire this virtuoso ability, which is partly inborn anyway?

The second way is by smell. This is more in the amateur's line. Silver, if vigorously rubbed with a piece of woollen rag (or the cuff of your jacket) or the palm of the hand (spit on your hand first, if you like), gives off a highly characteristic smell. You can easily familiarize yourself with this smell by practising on a piece which you know to be genuine.

How to clean silver

The air of towns and cities, which contains sulphuretted hydrogen, rapidly tarnishes silver. Eggs and cabbage both turn silver black because of the sulphur in them. But however glaring this oxidation may be, it never goes deep and is easy to remove.

Commercial polishing pastes, whether sold for copper, brass, silver, aluminium, tin or pewter, are a little too abrasive to be recommended for frequent use.

However, you may find them extremely useful for pieces which have been neglected over a period of time, perhaps been exposed to harmful effluvia, and which have grossly deteriorated. We would like to persuade lovers of silverware that the finest lustre is often obtained by much gentler methods:

1. Lukewarm soapy water, stirred to a good froth, is very effective for cleaning silver which has merely turned black through use. A small amount of a powder detergent in very hot water will produce the same result without any danger to the metal.

After a thorough rinsing in hot water, vigorous polishing with a chamois leather will achieve the desired brilliance.

2. Alcohol is a perfect cleaning agent for all precious metals. With the addition of a few pinches of whiting (Spanish white) it becomes a cheap, simple mixture for reviving the brilliance of tarnished silver, even if the surface is slightly scratched (as is frequently the case with household utensils and with bracelets and rings, all of which are liable to take a knock now and then).

3. Cyanide of potassium dissolves the oxides of silver, but is much too poisonous to be considered for ordinary use.

4. Silverware hardly ever turns up in excavations, and when it does its care always constitutes a special case. It is regarded primarily as a piece of archaeological evidence; its appearance is a minor consideration. Only coins are usually cleaned in depth, to display their original brightness in numismatic collections. To achieve this result with grossly dirty items, sulphuric acid (vitriol), diluted with water, should be used, in the proportion of one part of acid to ten parts of water (add the acid to the water, not the other way round). Immerse the pieces in the liquid for a few minutes, watching the effect carefully.

5. Perfectly genuine silver sometimes shows traces of verdigris (a bluish-green patina), resulting, of course, from long exposure to a corrosive atmosphere because silver is almost always alloyed with a certain percentage of copper in order to give it the mechanical properties, including hardness, which pure silver does not possess.

The method for completely removing this surface copper is a trifle drastic, but very easily controlled.

Heat the article red-hot (but be careful: silver melts at 960 °C so don't use a powerful gas or propane torch; the ordinary domestic gas supply is quite adequate for the purpose; better still, use a barbecue stove). Whatever source of heat is used, the article will quickly turn black because the heat oxidizes the copper. At this point, *boil* the article in sulphuric acid diluted one part acid in ten parts water. The copper will disappear and the surface will be pure silver, which you can polish with chamois leather and whiting.

Folk recipes
Here are a few ancient dodges, in the old-wives' category; they work excellently, and are picturesque enough to tempt anyone to try them.

Powdered red ochre
Ordinary ochre, as used by house painters, bound with a little soap or vegetable oil, makes a very bland polishing paste for ordinary use.

Cuttlefish bone
Pick up the cuttlefish bones left by the tide on the beach. Cage birds love having them to peck at, but that isn't why we are recommending them. Pound them to a fine dust and use it for polishing your silver. The results are surprising.

Sour milk
Or, to be precise, skim milk. This provides a painless way of restoring the brilliance of any silverware which is suffering from mild neglect. Immerse the object in skim milk for a few minutes; when you take it out don't rinse it but let it dry on its own, then rub it up with a rag or chamois leather.

Do you want a patina?
This is popular on the continent but not in Britain. The blackening of silver, nicely controlled, makes an effective contrast for heightening the effect of relief or intaglio. Professionals use a liquid whose basic ingredients are alcohol and antimony. This darkens the silver; the parts in relief can then be rubbed with a

commercial polish or a little silk-fine pumice, to produce the light and shade that some amateurs particularly cherish.

Another very simple method: expose your silver to sulphur vapour and it will quickly turn black. Alternatively, warm the article and then dip it very briefly in strong bleach to achieve the same result.

16 Tin and pewter

Tin and pewter

Tin has always been a precious metal in a sense; perhaps the only one whose attractiveness was not reflected by its monetary value. Its price does not begin to compare with that of gold or silver. This may be regarded as a pointer to its intrinsic beauty, which was recognized from the infancy of the historical civilizations onward. Tin was loved for its own sake, not for its rarity.

For, if tin had not existed bronze would not have existed either, a deficiency whose consequences would have been incalculable. What would the civilizations of Egypt and Mesopotamia have left to posterity without the bronze tools of their sculptors? What would the earliest Chinese dynasties have bequeathed to us, those of the Yin period (fourteenth–eleventh century B.C.) without the admirable bronzes? What would we know of Mesopotamia, Nineveh, Babylon or the Persians, without the delightful bronzes of Luristan and the figure-sculptures of Sumer?

Who can measure the cultural content of the trade to which tin gave rise, thousands of years before the Christian era? It is an attested fact that the ore utilized by the peoples of Mesopotamia was mined in Galicia (Spain), and doubtless also in Britain.

The earliest objects made of pure tin that we know of are a ring and a pot found in an Egyptian burial ground of the eighteenth dynasty (about 1450 B.C.). No deposits of tin were exploited in ancient Egypt and it is not yet known whether the ore came from Syria, Spain or northern Europe.

In England, the organization of pewterers into guilds goes back to Saxon times, to the reigns of Athelstane, Alfred and Edward the Confessor, and in France the craft was of equal, if not greater, antiquity. For this, record is lacking, but it is a known fact that there were at least nineteen master pewterers thriving in Paris in the time of St Louis (1226–1270).

But to get to what concerns us here, let us telescope time and jump forward to the Middle Ages when pewter entered popular use.

In the fourteenth century, household vessels of wood and coarse pottery began to be replaced by pewter, which, in addition to its intrinsic value, had the advantage that it could be periodically renewed by melting down. This is the main reason for the rarity of really old pieces. The pewterers went round visiting households where they melted down and remade worn-out vessels for a modest charge, calculated by weight. To stimulate trade and keep up with fashion they modified the shapes in use. This is why *no* tangible evidence has come down to us of the pewterware of the thirteenth, fourteenth and fifteenth centuries, and only a few examples from the sixteenth and seventeenth centuries. In the eighteenth century we see a fairly large output, at which time the triumph of pottery and porcelain had initiated the decline of pewter. Relegated to the scrap-heap by nineteenth-century taste, these examples of a private, domestic art are now collectors' items.

Fakes

The incredible amount of fake pewter in circulation is not easy to study in the abstract, at second hand. Scarcity has always favoured counterfeiting; but these copies – of widely varying quality – are so numerous as to prompt the involuntary thought 'How is it that people who have chosen the honourable and beautiful trade of the antique dealer are capable of offering, to a reasonably informed public, a host of objects ordered from the nearest workshop?' If it is merely from financial necessity they should set up in some other line of business. They would do well out of souvenirs – the folksy doll or the barometer surrounded by seashells.

Some of these antique dealers say straight out, 'These are copies.' Their integrity does them honour; but all it means is that their vocation is not for the souvenir trade but for selling furniture and decorative goods.

If the profitability of the antique dealer's profession depends on the combination swindler/dupe, antique dealers will become extinct – with highly regrettable repercussions on our enjoyment, our way of life and art of living.

Nor are antique dealers the only culprits. What are we to think of the hacks who call themselves 'master pewterers' yet have never done anything but mechanical reproduction work, endlessly casting copies of forms created by others?

Pewter is a wonderful material; it has everything to attract a real artist. Such artists are few, and they are often denied the chief incentive possessed by the master-craftsmen of earlier days: utility. For, as we should remember, not a single pewter piece has come down to us that did not have an exact, daily, homely function.

Recognizing fakes

This needs much practice, and may prove a disappointing exercise at first, since a little knowledge is more dangerous than ignorance. The ignorant seeker can at least fall back on instinct.

First of all, carefully study pewterware known to be genuine in museums or the shops of specialized antique dealers, whose standards would not permit them to trade in dubious pieces.

What should be your guidelines in such an examination? Bear it in mind that pewter is a highly malleable metal, not to say soft, and that long use may have made its marks on the most carefully preserved object: slight dents in the foot, neck or lid of a wine jug or the rim of a dish, traces of cuts on a plate or a bowl, faint or marked deformations in the belly of a pot or a tureen.

Imagine centuries of patient care, ranging from ordinary cleaning by a kitchen maid to the thorough polishing administered by a critical housewife. Old pewterware has been used and looked after – and don't tell us that many years of subsequent neglect will have wiped out the consequences. Once you remove the dirt and oxidation which can dull the most brilliant pewter, the indescribable modelling peculiar to forms long caressed will reappear.

Fake pewter has sharp edges, even if care has been taken to disguise them. The care shows up and betrays the deception.

Even if the fake has been cast from an antique piece, the

modelling will have acquired a flabby quality. This is one of the peculiarities which invariably distinguish a cast copy. It shows up glaringly in the marks. The master pewterers, or in certain cases the controllers of weights and measures (wine mugs, for example, had to conform to an official shape), possessed steel punches with which they marked the soft pewter, placing it over a 'stake' (a kind of miniature anvil) to give a bearing for the hammer-blow and to prevent the pewter from being dented or bent.

On genuine pieces these marks are clear and sharp – or at least part of them is; the hammer didn't always come down quite flat. On the inner surface, opposite the imprint, the 'stake' will have left its own impression, something like a hammer mark. On a copy these marks are soft and blurred. They are like what you would get by pouring molten lead or tin into the impression made by a coin in wet sand.

More seriously, forgers have acquired the habit of using their own punches. What should alert you to these is that the edges of the imprint are *too* sharp, the sunk parts are free of the metal polish and oxide which the polishing rag could not reach.

Forgers do not neglect to use acid baths to generate spectacular oxidations, various concoctions to produce a spurious patina and so on. Common sense and careful observations are really your only guides.

It is worth pointing out that the presence of these punch marks proves nothing; countless genuine pieces are without them!

Finally, we can only urge the amateur to educate himself; there are excellent books which teach the language of punch marks and show how the forgers have been at pains to imitate the best known marks, such as the famous 'rose and crown' which, when genuine, has so many variants that even specialists get confused. It helps a little to know that certain master pewterers, such as the famous Bartholomé Leboucq of Lille, used five different punches which included versions of the rose and crown; so did his competitor, Lefebre. To confuse the matter nicely, we add that the celebrated rose and crown is also found on pewter from Brussels and Liège.

The marks and what they express

Without trying to make oneself into a walking encyclopaedia of punch marks – which would be impossible, because there are still so many to be discovered and classified in many countries – it is a good thing to know the meaning of the most eloquent types of mark one is likely to encounter in France and England, where perhaps old pewter is understood and collected more seriously than anywhere else.

Master craftsmen's marks on pewter

Guild organization in both England and France in the Middle Ages is well known: it meant that every pewterer could put his own mark on his wares, provided he was accepted by a jury of guild masters. The craftsman had to conform to certain standards, notably as regards the quality of his alloys. The corporation (guild) then considered itself responsible for the standard of what he produced.

According to law, every master pewterer was required to incorporate his initials in his personal mark. In some cases the whole name is given or is represented by a kind of visual pun. Several instances are known in which the name is depicted analogically. Edward Groves of London used the device of a man's figure walking through a grove of trees.

However, literal initials are by far the commonest form, accompanied by a hammer as emblem (a pewter-beater's hammer, with a peen at both ends). The famous rose and crown belongs to London as well as northern France; the equally famous 'angel weighing a soul' (if that is what it really is) or 'angel with the scales', to eastern France (and Lyon); name-pictures and similar graphic devices, chiefly to Paris (which itself is usually denoted by the letter P). An act of parliament in 1641 enjoined the use of the thistle by all Scottish pewter masters.

Where are these punch marks placed?

Usually on the outside of the bottom of dishes, miscellaneous utensils, and wine pots and wine jugs. In both of these latter, the marks may be on the lid.

In English, marks are known as 'touches'.

Standard marks

As we mentioned, the guild *jurés* in France took responsibility for
the alloys used by the members of the guild. Naturally they kept a
check on standards. These standard marks are easily recognizable.
They are never more than a centimetre across, and they embody
either the letter F (often a double F, or sometimes two F's back to
back with the uprights coinciding), standing for 'fine' pewter, or
a C (often double, sometimes back to back or interlaced) for
common pewter. Of course there are variants: a coat of arms, a
town's name, date, the quality of the pewter spelt out in full and
so on.

There was no comparable system for standard marks in
England. The guild mark of Rose and Crown was by way of
certifying to the purchaser that the pewter was not below a
certain standard of alloy and weight laid down by the law. There
are therefore fewer 'touches' to be found on English pewter. An
X mark, with or without a crown, was in early use to denote
'extraordinary ware', i.e. of very high quality alloy, but abuse of
the mark led in time to its becoming valueless as a clue to quality.

Measure marks

These concern us only when they occur on pewter vessels used as
measures, notably wine pots, which were periodically checked by
a visiting inspector of weights and measures. The marks are small
signs placed on the lid or at the top of the neck. In France they are
astonishingly varied; the systematic classification of them, though
courageously undertaken by experts like Charles Boucau in Paris,
is continually being augmented by newly discovered types.
English measure marks are, again, not so complicated, consisting
of the amount of the measure, the date punched, and a punch to
indicate the reigning monarch.

Owner's marks

These are very rare, and should not be confused with the incised
initials, symbols and blazons which are fairly common on pewter.
Owners' marks are stamped: they are punch marks and can
clearly be seen to be so. Presumably they were put on for the same
reason as hotel keepers put '*Hôtel des Voyageurs*' or '*Restaurant de la*

Plage' on their china and ashtrays. Known examples include the *Hospice de Beaune*, the *Hôtel royal des Invalides*, a number of religious communities and hospices, and certain others which are hard to identify but probably represent ecclesiastics or ordinary private owners.

Countermarks *above:* Medallion type *below:* Rose-window type

Countermarks

These are not punch marks in the usual sense but lozenges or other marks in relief; one finds them, especially in pots, on the inside – for which reason they usually go unnoticed. The signs they contain, such as initials, dates and decorative designs resembling rose-windows, are difficult to interpret. Their presence is due to a technical reason. Until the eighteenth century, pots were cast in two-piece moulds; the two parts, and any roughness in the join between them, were then smoothed on the lathe.

The pot was held in a mandrel and presumably by an opposing threaded part passing through a hole in the bottom.

The countermark was a stopper, soldered into place, closing and camouflaging the hold left by the mandrel.

So the importance of the countermark is obvious: it is a sure indication that the piece was made before the eighteenth century.

Tin and its alloys: varieties of pewter

The following were the three officially recognized grades of tin and pewter used by the master pewterers:

Tin and fine pewter

This was probably pure tin with the addition of some substance (possibly bismuth) to facilitate casting. Pieces made of this material are extremely rare and are mainly fine table vessels (tureens, ornamented soup bowls and the like), for which ordinary pewter was also used; organ pipes, theoretically, had to be of pure tin, were likewise made of either material; the distinction is evidently difficult to draw in many cases.

Common pewter

Any attempt to estimate the composition of the metal is risky, as it was common practice among the master pewterers to melt down old tin or pewter. It was even recommended not to use less than one-third of old metal when casting new pieces. Besides, each master had his own secret formula for the additives to be used: copper (*cuivre rosette*, as pure copper was called), bismuth, metallic oxides, antimony, tungsten and so on.

Ley (la claire étoffe)

In this very inferior quality there was no check on the amount of lead. The pewterers, well aware of the poisonous properties of lead, were careful not to use ley for anything which might have to contain food or drink. It was used for clysters, cheap candlesticks, candle moulds and other prosaic purposes. It should be remembered that as well as the pewterers there were large numbers of tin and lead founders whose guild was not governed by regulations controlling quality. Ley is a heavy metal alloy in the proportions of approximately eighty parts tin to twenty parts lead.

Silver pewter

Pewter, if well enough polished, gleams in simular a way to silver, giving rise to a legend whose motivation is strictly commercial: the existence of silver and tin alloy. Technically, at least, this is feasible despite the different melting points of the metals (tin, 232 °C, silver, 960 °C). Reasons of a different kind make the alloy improbable. A cause frequently adduced for the popularity of pewter is the sumptuary edicts issued in the closing years of Louis XIV's reign (there were others later), penalizing the 'outward signs of wealth' symbolized by the possession of silverware. But it would have afforded little satisfaction to the proud owner to bury part of his riches by alloying it with a metal of a baser kind. Moreover, in order to succeed in alloying silver and tin the pewterers would have needed more heat than was generated by the braziers illustrated in the technical treatises of the time. These were fired with charcoal and are unlikely to have produced temperatures above 600–700 °C: this argument is not necessarily conclusive; and the goldsmiths and silversmiths may well have resorted to working in less precious metals, including tin. Why, however, should they have used this particular alloy, which would have contributed very little to the characteristics of its principal ingredient, tin. The presence of silver in pewter is said to be proved by certain highly characteristic oxidations reminiscent of frost-patterns on window-panes in winter. But surely this is one of the typical oxidations of tin? However, to avoid discouraging the partisans of the 'silver pewter' theory we will concede that common pewters did contain a certain percentage of silver, because they contained lead – about 10–20 per cent of it; and galena, natural lead sulphide, the principal ore of lead, always includes a certain amount of silver.

How to recognize pewter

This is chiefly a matter for the eye and cannot be described in words. There are other tests; smell is one of them: pewter rubbed with a cloth, or even the palm of the hand, gives off a character-istic odour. However, the objection will be raised that all metals do this more or less; or at least that silver and lead do. Another test is the sound, the peculiar note or 'cry' of the material. The 'cry' of pewter is a cry of pain. The metal's markedly crystalline nature engenders a clearly perceptible effect: if pewter is slightly but forcibly twisted, an unmistakable creaking sound will be heard; a 'cry' produced only under torture. Consequently this test cannot often be used!

Pewter pathology

Pewter has its own sickness; some grave, some even mortal. But before embarking on this distressing subject it is fitting to draw attention briefly to the health-giving properties of pewter. It is lethal to staphylococci. It can be plausibly argued that the pewter vessels use in hospitals from the Middle Ages to the end of the eighteenth century were responsible for largely suppressing the 'ward fever' which is still a scourge even today, in this age of organ transplants and pacemakers for the heart, and which is caused by an uncontrollable outbreak of the 'hospital staphylococcus', *Staphylococcus doreus*, against which modern asepsis is powerless. Tin, like silver, has bactericidal properties; in various forms it is an ingredient in ointments and other local applications, and is used in the treatment of boils, anthrax, influenza and even tuberculosis.

Pewter's 'cancer'

We mentioned, in discussing 'silver pewter', an oxidation resem-bling hoar frost. It is sometimes referred to as 'pewter's cancer'. This sinister title is highly exaggerated. Crystallizations of this kind are undoubtedly hard to get rid of but do not eat away the body of the metal. A fine pewter vessel can always be restored to its proper brilliance; the sensible thing is to treat both the object and its material with respect, starting with gentle remedies and gradually adopting severer ones if necessary.

Simply use a commercial metal polish, rubbing hard and con-centrating particularly on the oxidized patches. Wipe clean and shine now and then, to check results. If these promise well, con-tinue; the method is both right and safe.

A very dirty article, apparently oxidized in depth, can be immersed in paraffin (kerosene) and left there for several hours or even days.

It should then be dried with newspaper (which is highly absorbent); probably all the accretions will come away easily. Finish by polishing with a cloth and any of the usual metal polishes.

Another method, which sounds even more home-made, is the 'hay bath'. Take a metal pan or pot, place a few handfuls of hay in it and put the object on top of the hay; fill the pot with enough water to cover the object. Heat the pot, bringing the water not quite to the boil and leave it to cool; after a few hours most of the dirt will have gone.

Potash, soda and ammonia all possess the property of precipitating the salts of tin. Any of these three will easily eliminate the most tenacious oxidations. But care is necessary. Rinse the pewter thoroughly as soon as you see that the action has gone far enough.

Dilute hydrochloric acid is sometimes recommended for cleaning pewter, but this is a serious mistake: tin is dissolved by hydrochloric acid. Of course, this treatment quickly gets down to the bare metal but, in our opinion, gravely compromises the appearance of the article by destroying the patina.

The patina of pewter does not depend on preserving the blackish oxidation covering its surface. Specialists all agree that pewter should be clean and brightly polished. Motifs, mouldings, channellings and engraved details are bound to show differences of colour; this is desirable because it brings out relief and modelling and thus shows up the line of the object as a whole.

Pewter's worst 'disease'

The most serious trouble that pewter can develop is a 'disease' essentially due to *cold*; deep ulcerations or erosions appear on the surface and these miniature craters contain powdery salts of tin, showing that the metal has literally decomposed. These attacks may be local; unfortunately, they may on the other hand affect the whole surface. What is to be done? The question causes much argument, and more perplexity, among specialists.

In the case of a valuable, old piece, especially if it is badly attacked, the current trend is to let well alone, merely cleaning up any portions still intact with metal polish. The true amateur will cherish the article for its historical significance and be content to forgo its decorative qualities – but he will also be compelled to witness the further progress of the 'disease'!

However, if action is not taken in time, the deterioration will obviously become general. It is advisable first carefully to scrape out the 'craters', then to take chemical action against the salts produced by oxidation. As we mentioned, these can be eliminated with soda, potash or ammonia. Finally, after polishing as thoroughly as possible, apply the following which, in spite of its simplicity, is acknowledged the best by the most advanced metallurgical laboratories in the world. Heat the article, within reason, and coat it with a substance produced by nature: beeswax. The wax melts on the hot metal and sinks into the minutest cavities of the surface, envelops the oxides and gets right down to the metal itself, isolating it from the oxygen of the air and rendering impossible any further spontaneous chemical or molecular reaction. Carefully wipe off any excess wax, and polish. This 'proofs' the article permanently.

But, if your pewter is exposed all over again to the rigours of climate and atmosphere, no panacea will safeguard it from damage.

Beeswax or the atom?

Anti-corrosion treatment with beeswax is a simple common-sense remedy, the effectiveness of which is based on an observation frequently made. Whenever excavation has yielded receptacles which once contained unguents or cosmetics – every civilization has bequeathed us items of this kind – these receptacles have been preserved intact, without serious deterioration, despite having lain underground in damp or acid conditions. Analysis of ancient beauty products regularly indicates the presence of beeswax. It even seems that beeswax has been recovered intact from fossil deposits dating from early periods in the earth's geological development.

The idea has occurred to some people that radio-activity could be used to arrest oxidation. The British Museum entrusted a fairly large collection of coins to the British Atomic Energy Commission.

After treatment, the coins were found to be emitting highly dangerous gamma-radiation and the collection was placed in lead containers, to be stored for centuries in a specially adapted cellar at the Museum; where, of course, it can be neither handled nor seen.

Healthy pewter

This review of pewter might lead one to suppose that it is fated always to be attacked by dreadful maladies. Far from it, there is also a paradise for pewter – the safety ensured by vigilant, regular care. It is worth recalling that the Catholic Church admits the use of pewter as a sacred metal; a venerable distinction to which we are indebted for various objects full of grace, such as ciboria and small vessels for the holy oils. A further advantage is that we make use of the recipes for polishing pewter which an old maid-servant in a curé's household will be able to supply, and which are equally useful for all kinds of pewter. Apparently, pumice powder is the material to which the care of pewter has been entrusted for hundreds of years. Traditionally it is mixed with olive oil, a dab of the mixture put on a cloth and rubbed till the job is done. You can get pumice powder from specialized firms serving french polishers and cabinet makers. Ask for the finest grade. Spanish whiting mixed with ammonia is another standby, tripoli is another; so is the cabinet makers' *popote*. In France, excellent *popote* can be bought, whose ingredients are scientifically balanced. Every antique dealer or cabinet maker has his own recipe, but these are not to be trusted. Most polishing pastes include the ingredients mentioned above and are therefore the best answer to your problems. But, do not let whitish deposits of paste accumulate in the crannies and undercuts; take a hard brush, a paint-brush if need be, and lightly whisk them out.

Pewter, which is a soft metal, has anti-friction properties, like antimony or bronze. But whereas a pointed tool easily scratches it, the friction of cleaning does not wear it away as much as might be expected. How does one get a really good shine – given that all polishing is a process of controlled wear? As already stated, genuine antique pewter has an inimitable patina. Various drastic methods have been recommended: pads of steel wool, soaked in paraffin or oil, or, more recently, the plastic saucepan scourers used by housewives. We regard such methods as brutal and unsuitable. They do make pewter shine but work rather like glass-paper, that is to say by cutting microscopic glittering grooves in the bare metal. This is nothing like the matt, satiny gleam produced by gentle polishing.

Mechanical polishing is decidedly more attractive. An almost perfect patina can be obtained by using a felt or fabric disc and smearing it from time to time with a cake of solid polishing paste. But this takes a long time, because of pewter's low coefficient of friction. Fast running is essential: not less than 2500 r.p.m. The small discs supplied for the do-it-yourself having electric drills are inadequate, having too small a diameter to be sufficiently flexible, and the metal mounting in the centre of the disc too easily comes into contact with the pewter, and may mark it. But if you possess a buffing wheel you can run it off a d.i.y. drill and there is nothing to stop you from equipping it with a felt disc 15 to 20 cm in diameter.

For those who prefer dark pewter

Pewter can be left coated with a thin layer of oxide. The metal can first be smoothed by light polishing, then hot-waxed. A good rub thereafter will produce a high gloss.

Paraffin (kerosene) or vaseline can be used instead of beeswax. And there is a popular recipe which is very sound: rub the pewter with a cloth dipped in hot beer, and simply leave it to dry. Take care not to use too harsh a cloth when polishing it. A piece of soft knitted woollen material will polish up the film left by the beer but will not remove it.

Repairing pewter

This is undoubtedly a job for the specialist. It is a very difficult matter to solder two metals which have the same melting-point: in melting the solder one runs the risk of melting the metal under repair as well. This could be disastrous. The most the amateur can attempt is to stop a hole on the bottom of a plate or dish, using an electrician's soldering-iron. Never try to melt the metal of the article itself; simply put on solder, after cleansing the edges of the hole with hydrochloric acid. Excess solder can be removed by filing, followed by emery cloth, then gradually polished up with wet-and-dry and finally with metal polish.

Filling a hole or crack without soldering

It is always possible and requires no particular skill. A vase or a teapot may, after long use, show signs of weakness round the bottom, or at the base of the spout, or in the handle. Two-part epoxy resins will permanently repair these little defects. The resin's resistance to heat, 300 °C is about 68 °C higher than the melting-point of pewter. The plastic pastes with a metal filler ('cold solder' or 'plastic metal') may be helpful in small repairs. Be prepared for its limitations, however: you may not be able to match the colour exactly, or to polish the finished join satisfactorily. Don't expect a high finish: the repair will always present a comparatively dull surface. So keep this method for places that cannot be seen.

Taking dents out of pewter

Here you will need a selection of the tools used by a panel beater or a tinsmith (they are much the same); namely: a round-headed hammer, a mallet of wood or hard rubber and a 'universal' former (a metal object whose faces have different curves). If you are not going to need this equipment often, rent it. But the mallet is indispensable.

Get your hand in first by working on an old tin, first bashing it up a bit, or on some white-metal article of small value. The principle is straightforward. You have probably watched panel beaters at work: they do not merely hit the inner side of the dent, because the impact which caused it also had the effect of stretching the metal so that knocking out the dent from one side would simply set it up again on the other. The knocking-out must be 'backed up' by holding a metal object against the face of the pewter exactly opposite the hammer or mallet striking the other side. This metal object is the former and it must be the same shape as the object being repaired. If you haven't got a former of the requisite shape you can make one yourself out of hardwood. If you need both hands for working with, you can fix the former in a vice. This, however, is not ideal; a certain amount of 'give', to take the impact of the hammer, is desirable.

Let us consider a few concrete examples. Anything *flat* should be laid on a perfectly flat surface, such as a table top or a bench top, and hammered into shape, with a piece of perfectly flat wood between itself and the hammer.

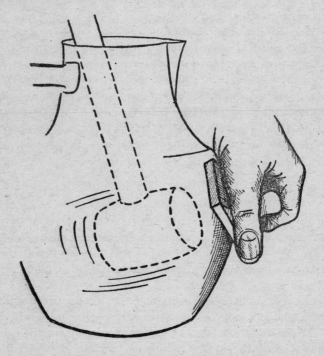

Anything *hollow*, such as a vase or a jug, should be beaten out from the inside, with a suitable former held against the outside. The pewter should be hammered with light blows accurately applied. To enable you to work effectively from the inside the hammer or mallet should be a small one.

The *foot* or *base* of any article should be treated in the same way: hit from inside, backing up with a wooden or metal former of exactly the right shape.

Some final hints

Pewter articles look well behind glass, or on a whatnot or other piece of furniture, or hung on hooks, or simply used for their original purposes. However, it is advisable to stick a felt pad (self-sticking) underneath to protect both them and the furniture from scratches.

Engraved or carved pewter is cared for just like all other pewter, with special care to brush out any residues of polish after cleaning.

Pewter vessels can be used for holding hot liquids. Teapots and chocolate jugs are often made of pewter; so are potpourri jars (big-bellied pots in which an infusion was made of supposedly sweet-smelling plants or substances, with the intention of perfuming the room – a dubious enterprise). No pewter vessel should be placed directly on a gas-flame or the red-hot element of an electric cooker; at most, it can be stood on a radiator or the protective plate at the top of a solid-fuel stove.

17 Tortoise shell

Tortoise shell

It seems that tortoise shell was an unknown material to the craftsmen of the Western world until the late fifteenth century; it was
introduced into Spain, Portugal, Italy and, subsequently, England, by the world navigators whose newly invented magnetic
compasses had enabled them to push back the frontiers of the unknown.

Apparently, however, the ancient Greeks and Romans had not
only been familiar with tortoise shell but had probably used whole
carapaces for making musical instruments – lyre, lute or cithara.
But what they probably used was the shell of the land tortoise,
common in all the Mediterranean countries. Only the marine turtle
concerns us here, the source of tortoise shell as we know it, that
precious and noble substance. The Renaissance cabinet makers
used it a great deal for encrusted decoration on cabinets and small
chests; after falling rather out of fashion in the early seventeenth
century it reached its peak in the eighteenth, achieving fame for
all time. In the reign of the *Roi Soleil* (Louis XIV) André-Charles
Boulle created an authoritative style with his furniture embodying
brass-and-tortoise shell marquetry. It is no exaggeration to say
that this was an official style, one whose florid ornamentation was
perfectly adapted to the Versailles of Louis XIV. Tortoise shell
has always been much prized in England but was never quite so
much used in furniture as in France. Supplies of tortoise shell
have always been available to English craftsmen, in small quantities at first, but in ever growing quantity as colonial expansion
in the Caribbean brought trading vessels, privateers, slave traders,
and later ships of competing nations into the area. Tortoise shell
also emerged in a triumphant profusion of such things as *boîtes à
mouches* (little boxes for containing beauty patches), fans, combs,

snuffboxes, frames – a field in which, from the late seventeenth right through the whole of the eighteenth century, the French have never been excelled, except perhaps by the Swiss in the early days of the nineteenth century and the house of Fabergé in the nineteenth century. The popularity of these articles was also the signal for the appearance of the earliest fakes. Powdered tortoise shell was bonded with gelatine or bone glue to look very like the real thing, a practice encouraged by the fact that moulded copies of the forms in vogue could thus be produced in large numbers. However, this may not have been intended to deceive. It is a reasonable supposition that craftsmen were still groping for the technique of working in tortoise shell; it was not until much later, in the Second Empire period, that they discovered how to weld it (joining it by heat, as described below), a process apparently unknown in the eighteenth century.

A number of famous collections contain genuine eighteenth-century pieces which are simply powdered tortoise shell stuck together with gelatine. This does not lower the value of the pieces in question; but it does impose on us the need to be highly circumspect in the matter of restoration.

After being slightly neglected in the opening decades of the nineteenth century, tortoise shell recaptured public favour when, under the Third Empire, the colonialist fever took hold of France, though the advent of celluloid soon brought severe competition.

Today, the subtle transparencies of tortoise shell are imitated with unprecedented perfection by the plastics industry.

But this does not destroy the refined pleasure a collector feels in the possession of objects whose value is known to himself alone.

The marine turtle

This creature is a native of the warm seas of the world. Though widely distributed in the Pacific and Indian Oceans, it is in the Caribbean that it supports large-scale operations, notably in the Bahamas, which yield the celebrated pale tortoise shell. The animal is by no means a marine monster – it weighs at most 50 kilos. The *'caret'* turtle, which is very common, is perceptibly different; its scales are what is called *tuilées* and are browner, sometimes almost black, and coarser in texture. Their market value is almost exactly ten times less than that of 'blonde' or 'demi blonde' tortoise shell. But they are much heavier: a *'caret'* turtle may tip the scale at 200 kilos or more.[1]

There is no satisfactory way of removing a turtle's carapace. The natives in the South Seas surprise the reptile when it is busy laying its eggs on a sandy beach, turn it on its back and light a fire over it. This makes the scales easy to detach. It must be pointed out that the turtle's carapace, though rigid, is not all in one piece but is an articulated structure.

The back is composed of thirteen principal scales with a border of subsidiary scales of a different shape; the belly, which is almost smooth, is always relatively thin. Fire has the drawback of damaging the carapace to some extent, and the method preferred when possible is to place the animal in boiling water. The death throes of the marine turtle are long, few creatures in nature being endowed with such tenacity of life. In the fisheries of the Seychelles, Madagascar and the Bahamas, which manufacture the famous turtle soup and sell it all over the world, the turtles are disembowelled and the meat is cut out in lumps from the natural receptacle formed by the carapace; and until the last moment when the last pound of flesh has been extracted, the heart, in a horrifying pool of blood, continues to beat and flutter. Only a reflex, perhaps; but how do we know? It is a pity that turtles are not as appealing as baby seals – which (especially if one presses the comparison home) they decidedly are not. Some skilled practitioners in the Caribbean even manage to strip the turtle without killing it; they throw the naked reptile back into the sea, and provided no barracuda, shark or other predator snaps it up, it grows a new shell. Experts are not deceived by this spare tyre, as it were, whose quality never equals that of the original. One cannot help thinking that some of these poor creatures must have undergone the same treatment several times.

Identifying tortoise shell

The material varies too much in appearance to be fully described and no reliable standards can be given for identifying and dis-

---

1. Pale tortoise shell may fetch 600 or 700 francs a kilo; ordinary brown tortoise shell, only 50 or 70 francs.

tinguishing it from plastic imitations. It varies in quality from black to pale.

Mediocre grades are rather opaque and are brown or black with lighter, translucent veins. An intermediate quality is 'cherry', in which the marbling is unobtrusive and the colour comparatively homogeneous. A whole gamut of different marblings can be observed, shades of the most valuable and highly sought after coalescing into a tint whose wonderful transparencies recall the varying nuances of amber. To decide whether a piece of tortoise shell is real or imitation, only your eyes can tell. Without special training, no one can claim the piece to be genuine. The imitations are virtually identical. Heating an object to detect whether it is made of plastic is unreliable (because some plastics don't melt), and may cause pointless damage. The only rational recommendation is to buy tortoise shell from a specialist.

Repairs to tortoise shell

Tortoise shell is a living substance which has the surprising quality of being susceptible to contact welding.

Tortoise shell has often been compared with plastics, and, like synthetic resins, it is softened by heat. The craftsmen of the last century plunged it into boiling water to which they had added a glassful of olive oil. This method still serves, especially for treating a piece of tortoise shell which has become distorted. Put the piece in sufficient water to cover it, and bring the water to the boil. How long the piece should stay there it is difficult to say; the only guide is to examine it from time to time until it is comparatively supple. Provide yourself in advance with pieces of wood and weights or cramps to hold it in the desired shape, because tortoise shell quickly recovers its stiffness on being taken out of water. The difficulty of repairing tortoise shell arises from the shape of the objects to be treated – keeping them in the right position if curved throughout, or carved, or so slender as to be particularly vulnerable.

Here is the method for welding the material. First of all, smooth the surfaces of the break which is to be welded together again; the best way depends entirely on the shape and cross-section of the broken part. You can scrape with something sharp and pointed in the case of a broken rib in an eighteenth-century fan, or gently and carefully file the spine of a comb, or scratch the lid of a sand-box with a scarifier or '*vaccinostyle*'.[1] In all cases the scraping must be as invisible as possible, except where the break has previously been mended with glue when every trace of glue must be re-moved. The pieces to be welded must of course fit each other perfectly. To keep them in place, under uniform pressure, use elastic bands, bits of wood and so on, prepared in advance. Then surround the article with a wet cloth to all of whose surfaces you apply hot irons which have been brought to a red heat. If the article is a small one you can use two irons, one on top and the other below. Leave them in contact with the cloth until they have cooled. Probably the cloth will burn as the water dries out of it, but this doesn't matter. Make sure the cloth is thick enough but not too thick; you want to get as much heat into the tortoise shell as possible. If the weld fails, don't hesitate, try again.

Excellent results can be attained with small articles by trim-ming the break with a razor blade and fixing the two parts to-gether – small cramps are ideal for this.

You then place the whole thing in water and keep it on the boil long enough for the parts to fuse together. Cabinet makers, who still use tortoise shell, add a few handfuls of bay salt to the water; presumably in order to imbue the tortoise shell with its original element.

How to polish tortoise shell

Professionals polish tortoise shell by a method called in French '*au gras*', that is, using a polish with a greasy base mixed with very fine abrasive particles. The abrasive can be the finely powdered pumice ('silk pumice') which in Paris can be bought in the special-ized shops in the Faubourg Saint-Antoine and, in London, in the shops of the small jobbing jewellers in the Clerkenwell Road area. The base can be ordinary vaseline. The cabinet makers' *popote* also yields excellent results. Rub the article with a chamois leather pad dipped in the mixture from time to time, and finish with a

1. A small lancet, something like a pen nib, which can in fact be mounted on a penholder. Used by doctors for vaccinating, it is also widely used in printing and in retouching.

clean chamois leather. This method only applies to tortoise shell which has been scratched. To restore a piece whose surface has gone dull, rub vigorously with a pad of chamois leather or cloth (not fluffy) coated with glycerine.

Cleaning tortoise shell has nothing difficult or special about it; soapy water, followed by thorough rinsing, is completely effective.

18 Wooden statues

Statues

Strangeness is the keynote here; statues are a world in which art is synonymous with emotion. Every individual will seek whatever answer most satisfies his intelligence, but will not necessarily approach the truth. No statue leaves us indifferent; who has not felt the malefic power of an African or Polynesian idol, or responded to the serene ambiguity of a Buddha whose very pose constitutes a language; or the pathos of Christ on the Cross; or the elemental, pagan, prehistoric force of a Virgin and Child from Auvergne or Catalonia, combining the Oedipus myth of the mother with an idealized vision of fecundity?

Statues are not easy things to live with. Some people have a curious criterion for judging statues, claiming that while one statue has a tonic effect another is disturbing, and so on; individual sensibility being the only arbiter. A statue is never *only* a work of art. If any form were divested of its cultural content, how much would be left? Time and experience bring conviction, and teach us that there is no art without doctrine; more precisely, without a spiritual doctrine.

We may see this reflected in the customary classification of Western religious art into three main epochs:

the *centuries of faith*, characterized by the hierarchical serenity of Romanesque statues and the elegance and flexibility of the Gothic;

the *centuries of piety*, with the triumph of realism in the Renaissance and of Puritanism in the seventeenth century;

finally, the *centuries of devotion*, full of swooning Virgins, breathless bleeding Christs, gilded wooden clouds denoting Paradise, and the bearded God the Father whose blessing presides over the whole decadent pantheon – a decadence reaching its consummation in the mass-produced plaster casts typical of the most degenerate kind of religious art.

*

We cannot, in such a book as this, supply criticism for determining whether a statue is genuine or a fake. Such an analysis of sacred art would demand several generations of specialists and might even then defeat them.

Substantial works are available, especially on representations of Christ and the Virgin, which are crammed with erudition yet have by no means exhausted the subject.

The common denominators of the statues that concern us here are age and neglect. The reader will accompany us in studying how to cancel or mitigate not only the ravages of time but those perpetuated by dishonest or incompetent restorers.

A wooden statue attacked by woodworm

The attacking may not be recent and it may even be possible to assume that the insects have departed elsewhere. But if you regularly find wood dust round the base of your statue, treatment will be needed. Various commercial products, which are insecticides and fungicides at once, are available for you to choose from. Buy a sufficient quantity of a colourless one. Find a receptacle large enough to take your statue, either standing up or lying on its side. Pour in enough of the liquid (the product) partially to immerse the statue, and leave it until capillary attraction has drawn the liquid right into the wood.

Penetration may take several days; the colour of the wood will tell you how it is getting on.

Leave the statue to dry in a well-ventilated place before putting it back in its usual position. It will now be safe from further attack.

A wooden figure crumbling into dust

This is common enough with wood sculptures, especially with soft woods like lime (much used for sculpture) and even with walnut. The paint (polychroming) remains intact but the inside is like a sponge. This mainly happens with carvings which have been covered with a thin fabric as a basis for the polychroming;

a fairly common technique which seems to attract woodworm. The insect appears to have made its way in via the base; finding all other exits blocked by a thick armour of lime or plaster it proceeded to colonize the entire interior. An alternative hypothesis: a cloth covering was used only on softwoods, which are easy to carve – and whose tender grain is precisely what the woodworm prefers.

We have applied two methods to this type of case, with complete success.

1. A french-polishing mixture based on colourless shellac, heavily diluted: 1 litre of the mixture to 2 litres of spirit (alcohol). Put the wooden figure into a bowl and slowly inundate it with the liquid, giving the wood time to absorb it. (When absorption ceases, let the figure dry, which usually only takes a few hours; then, and not before, start again and continue until the figure will absorb no more.)

2. We acquired a special liquid from a firm serving dressmakers and fashion houses. This liquid, whose composition varies from one manufacturer to another but usually has a cellulose base, is intended for stiffening fabrics and more especially the straw used by hat-makers and dressmakers. It costs little, and is more convenient than varnish because it requires no mixing or dilution and dries almost immediately. It sinks into spongy wood in spectacular fashion. Don't be stingy; keep on pouring until the wood will accept no more. By this simple means you can preserve a figure which the slightest knock could have destroyed.

A mutilated figure

Many figures are in a mutilated condition; how much does it really trouble you? The reflex action of any specialist is to advise against restoration. There is a real danger of impairing the harmony of a figure-sculpture by inventing a missing limb or passage of drapery. The most one should do is to provide the piece with a base, if it really needs it. We are against any further addition, except where it is just a question of joining up; for example, when a fold in a garment is interrupted, or the tip of a passage in relief has crumbled away.

Various makes of plastic wood are on the market; properly

used, they can be satisfactory. They are composite materials, with
the consistency of mastic, and can be modelled. After hardening,
which is fairly quick, you can perfect the repair by sanding or
shaping the plastic wood just as if it were real wood. It is made in
various colours to match different kinds of wood.

In practice there are two things to note: the first is that plastic
wood, of whatever make, has poor adhesion and the repair may
come off in your hand while you are giving it the finishing
touches. Second, when plastic wood has dried you may find it
has shrunk, or that there is a good deal of cracking, if you have
used it too thickly.

When buying your plastic wood, buy the appropriate solvent
as well: alcohol or acetone, according to the make. Heavily
dilute a suitable quantity of the plastic wood with the solvent
until it is like runny honey. It will penetrate the wood more
efficiently and stick perfectly. Don't put on too much; leave it to
dry. On this foundation you can build up with plastic wood at its
normal consistency; it will hold well. Cracking can be avoided by
adding a layer at a time and letting it dry partially before adding
the next. Or you can let cracking occur and simply fill it in with
liquid plastic wood. If the repair is a big one reinforce it with
tacks or small round-headed nails, which will fasten the plastic
wood to the figure, or with pieces of wood, even quite sizeable ones,
as fillers; this is preferable, as it does not affect the figure itself.

*

Note: Two-part plastic wood has recently appeared on the market;
one part is epoxy resin mixed with sawdust, the other is the
hardener. This is excellent for certain purposes but not for restoring wood sculptures. It is difficult to shape because it is so
runny, and after polymerization it is a good deal harder than the
surrounding wood, which makes it awkward to work flush when
finishing. Finally, it seems that stain and polychroming do not
take well.

A more satisfactory answer is a home-made mixture of vinyl
adhesive and fine sawdust (of the same kind of wood as the sculpture itself). The sawdust produced by sanding is best, because it is
so fine; you will be able to get it from a joiner's or cabinet maker's
shop.

The mixture takes time to dry, but it sticks perfectly and its consistency is ideal for final tooling. Cracking and shrinking may occur; to obviate them, put it on in successive layers.

How to restore polychroming

If you have restored a painted sculpture you will have to paint the restored part to harmonize it with the rest. Use gouache and watercolour. This will give great flexibility in matching different shades of colour; and if you go wrong you can wipe it all off with a sponge and try again.

If the original polychroming has cracked here and there and you have to match it for body and thickness as well as colour, gouache by itself will fill the gap; it, too, will crack a little as it dries, if you have put it on very thick. The cracks are easily eliminated by an extra coat, or on the other hand you may prefer to leave them because they harmonize with the rest.

If the gap is large, mix your gouache or watercolour with a little plaster of Paris; better still is the cement paint used by decorators; the missing material can be built up in successive layers.

Laying bare the earliest polychroming

This is undoubtedly the slowest, most delicate task you can undertake. As we know only too well, pious but misguided zeal caused religious sculptures to be periodically refreshed with a coat of paint, the colours being arbitrarily changed to suit the sartorial taste of the time. In addition, the long-suffering sculptures have often been done up a bit for other reasons; in many cases they have been scorched by a candle, or they have fallen over, or an attribute has been added – many figures of the Virgin, for instance, have been 'scalped' in order to accommodate a crown.

Only a practised eye, the result of long experience, can tell you whether or not to try to get down to the original polychroming. There may be as many as three or four layers; nor is there any certainty that the deepest layer was contemporaneous with the creation of the work – there is no guarantee that the paint was not stripped at one time or another. There is also the possibility that the decision to repaint was not dictated by the whim of fashion but by deterioration of the original colouring.

Which solution shall one choose? Is it better to risk finding only the merest vestiges of the artist's own treatment, or to preserve a later, apocryphal polychroming?

Every case is a special case, there is no general rule. A work still wrapped in its own intrinsic and genuine aura is doubtless more satisfying to possess than a dolled-up version, a travesty. On the other hand, a repainted figure is tolerable provided its essence has not been betrayed. The decision is for you alone.

You have the choice of two methods:
The first is mechanical, and indeed manual; the second, chemical.

Method 1 requires a long, thin blade such as a surgeon's scalpel or an erasing-knife (as used on paper). Try to attach the paint at some spot where it has started flaking off; if possible, a spot which can't be seen; preferably towards the back, which in most cases was not painted. The *modus operandi* depends on the fact that, while each layer is stuck to the one underneath, it also retains its own consistency. With a sensitive touch, and above all with patience, use your tool to detach each layer in turn. You will progress only a few square millimetres at a time, perhaps even less, but the result is always excellent. *Warning:* don't try this method on figures on which fabric was stuck as a foundation for the paint; you will find yourself removing the first undercoat instead of saving the original top coat.

If you opt for this method, it will keep you busy for days. You should therefore confine each bout of work to a single small area such as a hand, a foot or some detail of the carving.

Method 2 demands less patience but much greater finesse and perceptiveness.

Use fine washing soda in the proportion of 200 grammes (two handfuls) to every litre of water. The proportion can be adjusted after trying the liquid on the back of the figure, or the underside of a fold of drapery, or some other place that is not normally seen.

Use artists' paint brushes of sufficient stiffness to penetrate everywhere. Begin by reconnoitring the ground: discover how many layers there are and decide which one you want to preserve. Put some of the liquid in a saucer and lay the figure flat before starting work, otherwise ugly runs will disfigure it.

As soon as the paint starts turning matt and the liquid starts picking up fragments of pigment, sponge the work clean before continuing. Work evenly; apply the soda solution only where necessary. The hollows, where it will collect, will of course be attacked more strongly than the protruberances and edges.

Rinsing at intervals, as required, carry on until you have reached the layer to be preserved. As soon as it starts to appear, reduce the strength of the solution to 15 grammes (about 3 teaspoonsful) to the litre; this will have the effect of freshening up the original colour. All that then remains is to rinse thoroughly, leave to dry, and finish off with a coat of virgin wax.

Commercial strippers are not to be recommended; most of them are too fierce for such selective, delicate work.

19 Wrought ironwork

Wrought iron

**Tell me if you like wrought iron,
and I'll tell you who you are!**
Few things made from an ordinary, everyday material succeed in
attaining such a pitch of visual and emotive power as wrought
ironwork. No species of ironwork is useless. Almost no forged iron
was originally intended as a 'work of art', a fact which gives
peculiar weight to our thesis that everything starts from the
tool; the tool is the source. . . The most directly utilitarian object,
its form, highly functional, has through the ages evolved into a
'work of art'. It is only recently that the lesson has been understood, with the result that the designer will be the man responsible
for determining the forms of the tools of tomorrow.

Meanwhile, however, iron is pursuing a somewhat uncertain
career. For every sincere craftsman there are dozens of hacks
churning out 'artistic ironwork': standard lamps, wallbrackets for
pots of flowers; 'horror on horror's head accumulating', encouraged by the owners of 'bijou country residences' who burden
the simplest wooden shutter with 'rustic' hinges and bedeck their
abodes with 'Venetian' lanterns painted with stove black, like so
many poisonous fruits, the products of some little cheapjack workshop.

*

Genuine forgework is always easy to recognize; all that is needed
is a little common sense. Down the ages, a block or bar of iron has
always had to be shaped – drawn out, flattened or whatever else
was required – with the hammer, so that the result always displays a certain slight irregularity, a perceptible modelling, even in
the most carefully finished work. Differences in volume are almost
always achieved by forging in one piece, i.e. from a single piece of

metal, not by joining several pieces together. Joins in ornamental work are made by 'fire welding' or 'forge welding'. The pieces to be welded together are brought to a strong heat, only just short of melting point; they are then laid together and hammered to make them unite. The result is an assembly with a certain very recognizable character. This is not easy to describe in words; let us therefore describe the opposition, the betrayers.

Autogenous welding

If you have ever watched a welder at work you will have noticed that while with one hand he guides his welding torch, in the other he holds a metal rod. The function of the rod is to melt in the

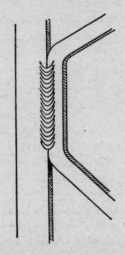

flame and deposit molten metal at the site of the intended weld. The method leaves easily discoverable traces: successive ripples, in a fairly regular pattern. Sometimes these markings are eliminated by filing but they can never be entirely erased.

Electric welding

Most of the producers of cheap 'artistic' ironwork, referred to above, use this technique. On the joints they make you will see one or two round beads, usually rather regular in shape. This is the sign of electric welding, or rather of the particular kind called 'spot welding'.

Riveting

This is not in itself a modern technique. Very ancient ironwork sometimes contains rivets or at least relies on the riveting principle, which consists of joining two pieces of metal by means of a cylindrical rod passing through a hole in each. The head of the rod, on both sides of the join, is spread out with the hammer; this is done hot. An extension of the technique is possible: the rivet need not be a separate component but can be part (not necessarily round, it may be square or oblong in section) of one of the two members which are joined together.

Nevertheless, amateurs are recommended to observe rivets carefully. Modern, industrially-produced rivets have perfectly regular round or flat heads, and hammering never quite disguises their character.

Two points for special emphasis

To the connoisseur, riveting commands less interest than work that is forged in one piece or fire-welded. This should not be taken as a hard-and-fast rule but as a general guide.

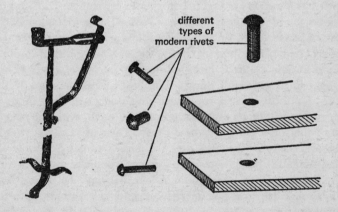

different
types of
modern rivets

The iron, or rather, mild steel, which is supplied by industry to the blacksmith of today is manufactured in shapes which make his work easier. For the genuinely creative worker this is all to the good. On the other hand, most of such craftsmen have observed that the composition of the present-day metal is by no means so suitable for fire-welding. The old metal ('wrought iron', in the metallurgical sense of the term) was softer; probably also less homogeneous.

The patina of iron and its language

Iron should not be masked by heavy layers of oxide, forming a nondescript blanket of patina, or, what is worst of all, smothered in stove black (Berlin black, matt black), as one has seen it only too often. Iron should display its own characteristic splendour; which implies that amateurs must use discrimination. For years, people have been polishing it up with grinding wheels; it is no longer possible to sell it with a natural surface – 'in its own gravy', as French antique dealers say. It is handed over for polishing and stripped naked. This is wholly to be condemned, and we shudder at the thought of a genuine example of beautiful ironwork being subjected to such treatment. It is all very well doing it to quaintly romantic bedsteads (which are usually cast iron, anyway), or the hooks, bars and so on from a butcher's shop, or obsolete agricultural implements, promoted to the rank of art works; but the imprint of time on wrought iron should be respected. Can you imagine the hinges on the doors of Notre-Dame gleaming like a lawyer's brass plate, or the admirable curlicues on thirteenth-century chests and cupboards in the Victoria and Albert Museum, or at Hampton Court Palace, polished up like silverware? Let us be loyal to the spirit of things. The blacksmiths who made the fittings for those chests, cupboards and doors attached them in their natural state, as they came from the anvil, with the roughness of the forge clinging about them. In many cases, wrought ironwork was polychromed and still shows traces of it: the so-called Armada chest, shop signs, some candlesticks, and probably fittings on furniture, were enhanced in this way. To polish them all is to sacrifice to a passing fashion and to eliminate both the patina and any vestiges of polychroming, thereby destroying irreplaceable relics of the past.

An expert will tell you that the patina and appearance of iron vary according to period and provenance. It can be argued that they do, but the margin of error is so great that one cannot lay down any classification even of the most vague and general kind.

Some patinas are black (without any assistance from black paint), others are more of a dark chestnut colour (notably in some Spanish ironwork), and there is an infinite variety of shades caused mainly by the condition of the metal: in ironwork which has been looked after correctly the patina will be transparent in places, with the grey gleam of the metal showing through; the same piece, if neglected – oxidized, eroded by time – or even cleaned by over-zealous hands, is likely to retain the reddish glow of rust here and there.

An observation worth mentioning is that *genuinely antique ironwork is comparatively immune to rust.* This may be the result of the precise amount of carbon and phosphorus present in the iron produced in past centuries. The gratings, balconies, rooftop ornaments, well-heads, signs and lamps which have resisted wind and weather for centuries have not been deeply affected by oxidation. Medieval locks on ancient chests *still work*, if one takes the trouble to have keys made for them (which is more than one can say for those of the last century, though admittedly these are more complicated).

Even more striking is the evidence provided by wrecked ships, still bristling with forged bolts, nails and ties which have remained almost intact, though the timbers have long since decayed.

The inference is that forged iron can stand up successfully to the passage of time provided it is not subjected to misguided interference.

How to clean wrought ironwork

This depends entirely on the degree of oxidation and the size of the object. The ideal is prolonged immersion in paraffin (kerosene), but this is not always practicable. Paraffin is one of the best substances, in all cases, for loosening rust, scale or dirt. It sinks through, by capillary action, to the metal itself; brushing afterwards is more effective.

Rusty iron can be heated and dipped in fuel oil or waste oil (e.g. from a car oil-change). With fuel oil there is of course the danger of its catching fire. Don't bring the iron to a red-heat, this is a mistake on two counts: it may ignite the oil, and it causes the iron to become mottled with unsightly marks.

'De-rusting' agents are inadvisable. They are powerful acids which do strip the iron bare but also attack the metal itself. This is a problem which the chemists will eventually overcome but at present it is not possible to recommend any of the products available for the purpose of cleaning antique ironwork.

Sand-blasting is also unacceptable. It wears down the surface all over, with aesthetically dubious results except for special effects. It should only be used on articles of little or no value.

Power-driven brushes: the wire brushes used for cleaning iron-work can now be electrically driven. This is a useful step forward. The brushes are of two kinds: those which spin in a plane at right angles to the axis of the motor, like a polishing disc, and those which work in line with the axis. They are much more effective than brushing by hand.

However, experience shows that they dull the surface of the iron to some extent. You can follow them up by using a soft polishing pad, also power-driven, combined with a solid polish. Hold the polish against the pad and give the latter a spin, so that it automatically gives an even, moderate coating of polish; then apply the pad to the iron. But remember the general caution given earlier: don't commit the blunder of polishing iron which was originally polychromed, or of destroying the character of forge-work by making it look like stainless steel kitchenware. The brushing and polishing described here are intended only to clean the iron and bring out its shape and character.

Emery cloth: this has always proved satisfactory for cleaning iron and it remains a standby. Obviously, being abrasive, it should be used in as fine a grade as possible, to avoid scoring the metal.

Steel wool: you may be familiar with this in the form of scouring pads for cleaning saucepans. Antique dealers use it continually for one purpose or another, and in particular for cleaning swords, bayonets, etc. and firearms; indeed, it is known in France as *'paille d'armurier'*, 'gunsmith's straw'. It can be used either dry or dipped in paraffin. While on the subject of weapons, it is worth mentioning that all the methods described here can be used with perfect safety.

Special care is needed to remove all traces of rust. If there is any pitting, a de-rusting agent can be applied, in moderation, to ensure deep penetration. So as not to overdo this drastic treatment, limit the amount applied by trimming a matchstick to a point and dipping it in the liquid, or use a toothpick in the same way. After the fizzing, which occurs instantly on contact with the dirty metal, rinse the liquid off and dry the work.

Protection with beeswax is excellent for swords, etc., but not so good for firearms, where it may cause the mechanism to clog. Use special gunsmiths' oil for these; vaseline is not permanent enough. Linseed oil has the advantage of 'feeding' the wood of the stock as well as protecting the metal, but it dries too slowly and may collect dust.

The preservation of ironwork
There is only one way of preserving ironwork without altering the appearance of the metal, namely *beeswax*. It is an advantage to heat the iron before waxing it, so that the wax melts on contact and gets right in everywhere. Wipe off any excess wax, let the iron cool, then polish with a soft cloth. No other treatment is worth mentioning; none yields such a satisfactory and lasting result.

Renewing a patina
If you have a piece which looks brand new, or one which has been mistakenly given a bright finish, there are various ways of darkening it.

Dip the article in waste oil, then heat it strongly until all the oil has disappeared. The result is a sombre patina of a dark grey, slightly bluish shade. Rub the object with a soft cloth and it will at once shine up beautifully. You can then wax it too if you wish.

An antique dealer's dodge which works very well: burn a pile of printed matter (old newspapers, magazines, posters, etc.) and hold the article to be 'patinated' in the flames. The vaporized ink combined with the lampblack deposits a film on the iron, which then merely requires waxing.

Shoe polish can be used instead of old oil; apply the polish, dry it out by heating the iron, and the colouring matter in the polish will be left behind (use black or dark brown polish).

Acid: on clean bare iron, acid vapours quickly cause the appearance of a delicate oxidation, almost powdery to the touch, which needs only to be waxed to become a brown patina. To obtain this effect, place the pieces requiring treatment in a confined space, such as a trunk or a cupboard, with a little ordinary sulphuric or hydrochloric acid in an open glass vessel. Don't leave them too long: twenty-four or forty-eight hours will be quite enough to oxidize the articles evenly all over.

*

We would like to end this chapter with a recommendation that you visit a museum where they have a good collection of wrought ironwork. The Musée Le Secq des Tournelles in Rouen is probably the best in the world. Others are at Hampton Court Palace and the Victoria and Albert Museum.

*

Note: Among the funerary equipment discovered in Tutankhamen's tomb was a dagger. This weapon was an eye opener to the experts. It is made of iron, whereas in the time of the Pharaoh in question the most currently used metals were copper and bronze. The dagger was entirely free from rust; a phenomenon correctly attributed to the perfectly dry atmosphere inside the tomb.

Theodora FitzGibbon
A Taste of Ireland £1·25

There is a flourishing Irish cookery tradition. Irish recipes are to be
found tucked away in odd corners of magazines and cookery books,
but many of these recipes come from private family papers which
have never before been published. They are accompanied by a
remarkable series of historic photographs.

A Taste of Scotland £1·25

The range of Scots cooking is wide, which is not surprising when one
considers the influence of Scandinavia and the 'well keipt ancient
alliance, maid betwix Scotland and the realme of France', which
inspires stovies, Lorraine soup, even haggis, not to mention Mary
Stuart's favourite biscuits. The photographs – from between 1845
and 1900 – cast their own poignant spell.

A Taste of Wales 95p

Here are many dishes whose Welsh names are themselves poetry:
Cawl Cymreig, Brithyll â Chig Moch, Pwdin Efa, Teisen Nionod . . .
'Once more Theodora FitzGibbon explores the food of another
country of Britain . . . authentic historical recipes are interleaved
with superb, touching photographs dating from the later years of the
nineteenth century' THE TIMES

A Taste of London £1·50

The food of London is as varied as its inhabitants and its history, and
Theodora FitzGibbon has mingled London's history with many
excellent recipes. The superb historic photographs give a unique and
touching insight into the bygone days of London.

A Taste of the West Country £1·25

'What a tasty dish! Dozens of them and all with regional connections
. . . Somerset braised lamb, clotted cream and syllabub . . . the
recipes for these and many more are presented, each facing a period
photograph' EXETER EXPRESS AND ECHO

British Architects and Craftsmen 85p
Sacheverell Sitwell

The author writes not only about Inigo Jones, Christopher Wren, Robert Adam and other great architects, but also includes the craftsmen – the clockmakers, silversmiths, bookbinders and the weavers of tapestries. He gives a complete picture of British taste and design from 1600 to 1830.

William and Mary £1·95
Henry & Barbara van der Zee

Charles II gave his blessing to the union of the soldier-prince William of Orange and the sensitive, romantic princess Mary Stuart, daughter of James II. A political expedient which turned into a love-match became a dynastic marriage of rare significance when William and Mary succeeded to the throne of England.

'The authors have made the whole period alive by vivid and relevant detail, descriptions of houses, clothes and habits'
BIRMINGHAM POST

You can buy these and other Pan books from booksellers and newsagents; or direct from the following address:
Pan Books, Cavaye Place, London SW10 9PG
Send purchase price plus 15p for the first book and 5p for each additional book, to allow for postage and packing

While every effort is made to keep prices low, it is sometimes necessary to increase prices at short notice. Pan Books reserve the right to show on covers new retail prices which may differ from those advertised in the text or elsewhere